# A Busy Day In Loafer's Glory

## A Rambler's Guide To Mostly Off-The-Path Carolina Places

### Mart Baldwin

Library of Congress Catalog Card Number  96-79547

ISBN Number  1-888549-01-7


Production Design by: Robin Ober

 APPALACHIAN PRESS
Nebo, NC  28761

Printer:    Professional Press
            Chapel Hill, NC 27515-4371


Manufactured in the United States of America
00 99 98 97 96              10 9 8 7 6 5 4 3 2 1

# *Preface*

People have different images of the wedge-shaped region that colors the map between Virginia and Georgia—the Carolinas, home of Tar Heels and Sand Lappers. Visions range from Scarlett O'Hara plantations to Tobacco Road shacks, from rhododendron in the clouds to alligator swamps. For some people our region is Mayberry. Others think of the rush and sizzle of today's Charlotte. Moonshine whiskey and mountain quilts tend to merge with new BMWs made in Greer.

All of these images are true, but the list is far from complete. The Carolinas wear many faces, and tell many tales.

Much of our country's history has been shaped by events—often bloody and violent—that occurred in the Carolinas. Just consider Fort Sumter. Or Kings Mountain and Cowpens. Or the Cherokees' Trail of Tears. Or even old Washington Duke's decision after the Civil War to start grinding tobacco in a shed on his farm.

How could a person even approach getting "to know" a place as wide and deep and old as the Carolinas?

Well, one way is to gather an armful of tourist brochures, study them, list all of the sites described, locate the sites on maps, work out an itinerary with a schedule and then just go. But if the region you are touring is the Carolinas, there are problems with this approach.

First, there are simply too many things to see. Your vacation—or even your retirement—wouldn't be long enough.

Second, you wouldn't be able to stick to your schedule; too many places would demand that you linger and learn. Third, even if you had enough time and stayed on schedule, you would miss many of the best places, the ones that aren't in the tourist brochures at all.

A better way to get tar on your heels and sand in your lap is just to start rambling somewhere and stop when you see something interesting. You won't have to go far. Spend some time getting acquainted with the place and the people there. Then wander on down the road to the next Carolina place and learn about it too. Keep going. There will never be an end to your ramble. This book describes 36 exploring trips through North and South Carolina that I took over a period of three years. Most of the pieces were published in *Carolina Senior Citizen* magazine as a column titled *Carolina Places.*

The tar on my heels is a little thicker now, my lap sandier, my tires a good bit more worn than when I started. I have seen much. But my list of Carolina places that I simply *must* get to know just keeps getting longer.

# Contents

# Howard Gap—Where A Boy Defeated A Nation

IN POLK COUNTY, NORTH Carolina, where I-26 passes through Howard Gap after its long steep climb up from the Piedmont, a monument stands on the east bank of the highway. A quick glimpse of the monument is all that a traveler gets, and no exit is there to permit a closer look. Over the course of a year many thousands of people must see the little stone column, but I expect only a very few know why it is there and what it commemorates. One bright May morning—my unmowed lawn and unplanted garden to the contrary notwithstanding—I decided to take the time to go to the monument and find out.

Avoiding eye contact with the exuberant grass of my front yard I drove the ten miles to I-26 in Hendersonville, then another ten miles on the Interstate, south. At the first exit north of Howard Gap—Saluda—I stopped at that ultimate tourist information source, a convenience store, for a pack of crackers and directions. The clerk didn't know what I was talking about, but a customer did.

"Just turn left there at Old Howard Gap Road," he said, pointing out the window to a side road that branched off from the Saluda highway just beyond the store. "Bear left at the fork, and keep going. You can't miss it."

Well, much experience has told me that I *can* and often do "miss it" after such directions, but since getting lost on a ramble is almost a goal in itself, I never hesitate. Today's directions were accurate. After winding four or so miles up a valley through crusty old apple orchards and yesterday's farms in the process of going back to being woods, the pavement stopped and the road became a cliff-hugging gravel lane sliced into the side of an almost vertical mountain. To my right the land fell away to a misty void whose bottom I could hardly make out. Happily, there were no log trucks on the road that day.

After another creeping mile I came back to I-26, where my road forked. The right fork, paved, led down the mountain. I kept to the left, crossed over the ever-busy highway with its endless hum of cars and groan of climbing trucks, and arrived at the monument.

At close range the thin gray stone obelisk looks like a just-sprouted Washington Monument. From a granite base, it presides over what might be all of South Carolina fading away to the east in a series of ever-lightening blue-gray ridges. The mountain peak that I had just crept around, Round Mountain, rises to the west of the Interstate. A bronze plaque set at eye level in the monument reads:

To Commemorate the Battle of Round Mountain in Which

CAPT. THOMAS HOWARD
and His Brave Followers with the Faithful Indian Guide
Skyuka defeated the Cherokee Nation
1776

In smaller letters at the bottom, the plaque tells that the monument was originally erected in 1909 by "Tryon Council No. 143, Jr. O.U.A.M." and that it was re-erected on the present site in 1967 (when I-26 was completed). The years of

Thomas Howard's life are given. He was born in 1760 and died in 1848. In 1760? That means he was only sixteen years old, already a captain, when he defeated a *nation* in 1776. Really?

Who was "Faithful Skyuka"?

What in the world is a "Jr. O.U.A.M."?

While I had been mildly curious about the monument before I read the plaque, I now *had* to learn more. The place to start learning about local things like monuments and battles is usually the closest library. Where would that be? From the monument I could just see the town of Tryon in the valley below me. I recrossed the Interstate, turned left onto the cliff-steep road that leads down the mountain and, in third gear, groped my way to the valley floor. I turned left again, drove a mile or two, realized I was going the wrong way, and turned around at Isothermal Community college.

A college called "Isothermal"?

A few minutes later I saw, in the center of Tryon, beside the railroad, a large wooden horse, white with black spots, wearing a hat.

A passerby gave me directions to the library. "Up there, just two blocks," she said, pointing across the railroad.

"And who is the horse?"

"That's Morris."

"Oh."

I spent the rest of the morning in the Tryon library and in the nearby town museum seeking the history of the nation-defeating young captain. The staff in both places was eager to help. I read much fascinating local history and posed for myself a page-long list of questions to pursue, but found only enough about Thomas Howard and faithful Skyuka to make me want to learn more. So during the next week I visited the Polk County Library in Tryon's sister town, Columbus, and spent a morning in the local history room of the Greenville (S.C.) County Library.

I found that not much is known about the Battle of Round Mountain. Most history books either don't mention it or tell little more than is given on the plaque. Apparently no one who fought at Round Mountain wrote about it (perhaps none of the participants could write), but from a few accounts dating from the last century I pieced together this story:

In 1776, after the Declaration of Independence, the sparse population on America's western frontier—the Blue Ridge Mountains in our part of the country—split between supporters of the King, Tories, and those who would in time be known as Patriots. Hostility grew quickly. The backwoods edged toward civil war.

The Cherokees watched and wondered if the time had come for them to strike back at the scourge of settlers that was steadily biting away the edges of their land. After much deliberation and dissension within their councils, the Cherokees joined with the British and declared war on the Colonies. Cherokee raiding parties, some accompanied by Tories dressed as Indians, fell on settlements up and down the frontier from Virginia to Georgia. They killed many settlers. Whole families were massacred.

In North Carolina, in the area below Whiteoak Mountain that would one day include the town of Tryon, the attacks were especially bitter. The Hite, Hampton and Hannon homesteads were attacked and family members killed. The raiders shot to death and scalped a farmer named Bishop and took his three children. (They were recovered six months later.)

In the Cherokee raids Tories were to be spared. A safety symbol called a "passover"—a peeled stick wrapped in white cloth—was to protect Tory households. Sometimes the plan failed. One Tory leader was killed while sitting beside his passover in his front yard.

After the initial Indian attacks all settlers who could moved to the blockhouse fort built a few years earlier just south of today's Tryon. (The blockhouse, restored, exists today as part of a private home.) News came that Cherokee raiders led by Chief Big Warrior, with Tory allies, had assembled in the forest to the west and were preparing to attack the blockhouse and sweep the area.

The men who had gathered with their families at the fort decided not to wait for the attack. Led by a young man named Thomas Howard they followed a Cherokee friend of Howard's, a brave named Skyuka, up through the gap that would one day bear Howard's name. They came during darkness on the unguarded rear of the Cherokee camp three or four miles from the blockhouse. A number of Indians were killed in the fighting that followed, which became known as the Battle of Round Mountain. Although they outnumbered Howard's force, the rest of the Cherokees withdrew, ending the threat to settlers in the region. According to an account published in 1897, rock mounds of graves where the Cherokees buried their dead after the battle were still to be seen on the farm of one Mr. Wash Fisher. They may still be there. I found no one who could tell me where to look.

So, who was Thomas Howard? What happened to him after the battle? Was he really just sixteen years old at the time? When did he become a captain? I found a few references.

Apparently he was a young hunter from nearby South Carolina who just happened to be in the Tryon area at the time of the Cherokee threat. I found no explanation for how he became the leader of the men in the blockhouse, most of whom must have been older than he was. Howard served for the rest of the Revolution in the South Carolina militia under

Colonel Benjamin Roebuck, where he attained his captain's rank.

After the war he lived out the rest of his long life as a farmer in Greenville County. A reference from 1897 notes that he was the father-in-law of "the late Elias Dill," but nothing more was said about Mr. Dill. An 1820 South Carolina census lists Revolutionary War veteran Thomas Howard, farmer, as a resident of Greenville County, his household comprising one female and three males. A book giving grave sites for Revolutionary War veterans states that Thomas Howard is buried in a family cemetery near Tigerville, S.C. I looked for the grave but didn't find it.

Who was Skyuka? According to legend, young Howard saved the life of the Cherokee brave after Skyuka had broken his leg when his horse, scared by a snake, threw him. (Another version holds that Skyuka was bitten by the snake.) Skyuka remained close friends with Howard and later betrayed his own people at Round Mountain. After that battle, legend also has it, the Cherokees caught Skyuka and hanged him beside a beautiful stream—Skyuka Creek today—close to where it joins the Pacolet River.

The "Jr. O.U.A.M." who paid for the erection of the original monument was the "Junior Order of United American Mechanics." I found nothing on why they put up the considerable funds to build the first monument, or what became of the organization.

The Battle of Round Mountain does not figure large in history books. But to the men following an Indian and a boy through virgin forests in the darkness of that long ago night to attack a larger band of feared enemy, the events must have loomed large indeed. Think about it next time you zoom along I-26 through Howard Gap.

# Do Bananas Grow In Tryon?

Tryon is in a climatic region known as a "thermal belt." For years I had heard accounts of perpetual springtime in the thermal belt areas on the southern slopes of the Blue Ridge, usually told to me at a time when my own place in the mountains was frozen solid.

What is a "thermal belt"? I wanted facts. How exaggerated are the isothermal tales I hear? Do bananas really grow in Tryon? I resolved to go there and find out.

Tryon and its companion town, Columbus, are easy to get to. Just on the North Carolina side of the N.C./S.C. state line north of Spartanburg take the I-26 exit for Highway 108, and turn west. You will come in about five miles, after passing the new buildings of Isothermal Community College, to Tryon. On the day of my visit I kept a sharp lookout for bougainvillea, orchids, parrots and other things isothermal and tropical as I drove.

Let me tell you right off, Tryon is *not* a tropical jungle. I saw no bananas or leopards. Or tropical snakes. What I *did* see on the blue and white morning of my visit were azaleas, including many of the yellow and orange flame varieties that shine like campfires in the woods, early mountain laurel, wild roses, honeysuckle, small wildflowers in profusion, and green everywhere. I'm sure that no jungle garden could have been as pretty as Tryon and its surrounding hills were on the day of my visit.

But I was there to seek information, meteorological facts, not to look at flowers. I began my serious technical questions with the waitress who served me lunch in a small restaurant on Main Street. She didn't have much to say about thermal belts but I learned other things.

Do you know that Tryon is round, a circle one and a half miles in diameter? It was laid out that way by the original surveyors. Or do you know why in Tryon's center stands the spotted horse, Morris? From my place in the restaurant I could plainly see Morris, who sported that day a black hat with a yellow ribbon around it.

I learned that Morris is the fifth generation Tryon Horse. He follows a line of noble ancestors which began in 1928 with creation of the first Morris, made for the Tryon Riding and Hunt Club by an organization called the Tryon Toymakers and Woodcarvers. A horse in the middle of town is appropriate for Tryon, since horseback riding and fox hunting are central features of Tryon life. I was told by my knowledgeable waitress to drive out of town on Hunting Country Road if I wanted to get the true flavor of Tryon.

I carefully followed her directions, got lost twice, then meandered for miles across the foothills south of town through a succession of horse farms. Rolling hills covered in deep, lush grass bounded by well-kept fences were populated with horses so beautiful they hardly seemed real. On each farm a large house was set on landscaped grounds usually filled with blooming azaleas. Most farms have names, often something involving foxes: Fox Hollow, Fox Trails, Fox Fields, Red Fox.

Signs along Hunting Country Road told me that something called FENCE maintained the trash-free condition of the highway. What could FENCE be? A mile or so further, just after crossing over I-26 for the third time on my ramble,

I found out. FENCE is Foothills Equestrian Nature Center, an organization which operates a nature preserve and throughout the year sponsors steeplechases, dressage shows and other horsey events. On the FENCE nature preserve are miles of hiking and riding trails.

Among the events sponsored by FENCE is the MOONHOWL, which occurs on September 21. I presume that the MOONHOWL involves horses, though I always thought it is wolves and coyotes that howl at the moon, not horses. Do foxes howl? In any case, horse-happenings occur regularly in Tryon. If you decide to visit the thermal belt this fall and happen to participate in the MOONHOWL, perhaps you could let me know what howls, particularly if it *is* horses.

Whatever howls are heard now will be much different from the war cries of Tryon's early history. The soft, civilized tone of the town today is far removed from the bloody time, before the American Revolution, when the Carolina foothills straddled the line that officially divided Cherokee land from white man's land, from the time of Thomas Howard and Skyuka.

The boundary line had been established by Royal Governor William Tryon, who made the long journey from Raleigh to the mountains and parleyed with the Cherokees to negotiate the boundary. Though the line became official, neither side paid much attention to it. Vicious raids going both ways—all, I imagine, accompanied by howls—were common. After the Revolution the Cherokees, who had sided with the British, were soon banished from their mountain home, and Tryon became a waystop for pioneers moving west.

Okay, fine. Tryon is a great town with a lot of history and many things to do and see, well worth a visit. But I wanted to find out about thermal belts. I wanted more information than my waitress could provide. I went back to the Tryon library.

9

I found that several scientific studies have been made of the thermal belt phenomenon, which is real but not quite of the magnitude of the legends I had heard. What happens is this: On clear nights, when there is much radiation cooling, the particular topography of Tryon and similar high foothills regions causes inversions. That is, the temperature at Tryon remains higher than that of land at lower elevations, sometimes by as much as 20 or even 30 degrees. Thus many frosty, fruit-killing nights in valleys below Tryon or on peaks above remain frost-free in the intermediate zone where Tryon is, the thermal belt.

But I still didn't see any banana plantations.

# Climbing The Wall At White Oak Mountain

A̶s I-26 approaches North Carolina from its sister state to the south, a vertical wall, a looming mass called White Oak Mountain, rises to block the way. The Interstate aims straight toward the mountain's heart. A first-time traveler will wonder if he is about to enter a tunnel. After the miles of smooth foothills to the south, White Oak is truly impressive.

Definite peaks mark both the western and eastern ends of the mountain. The silver thread of a long waterfall can be seen snaking its way down the south face, and, when the sun is angled right, windows in a row of buildings along the crest shine like lighthouse beacons. The trace of a road twisting its way up the mountain is visible from below.

At the last moment I-26 wisely zigs left to avoid collision, and ascends through Howard Gap, just skimming the western end of White Oak. I had followed the Interstate over this course many times, declaring to myself each time that someday I would take that wispy road to the top of the wall. On a cold bright day in early spring I did just that.

Leaving I-26 at the Columbus exit, I turned east onto NC 108, following directions in a Polk County brochure I had picked up earlier in the North Carolina Welcome Center. About a mile from the Interstate, in Columbus, Houston Road branches to the left toward the mountain. I took it, then turned right onto one of the several Skyuka Roads that I had seen in and around Tryon and Columbus. (I tried to keep count of the number of Skyuka roads, mountains, creeks and communities I saw on my foothill rambles, but soon lost track. I'm sure that the brave Indian companion of Thomas Howard would be pleased to know that he is remembered so assiduously two centuries later.)

Skyuka Road leads shortly to unpaved White Oak Mountain Road. From there, for the next four miles, the direction is *up*. On the spring day of my visit, "up" meant out of the fresh green, yellow and pink of spring and back into the gray and brown of winter. The road is rough but passable, and gets no worse as you climb. Houses at intervals grip the mountainside. Most appear to be summer cottages, unoccupied this early in the year, but others look lived-in. I didn't count the hairpins and convolutions required, but the road eventually reaches the top, where Sunset Rock, an outcropping at the crest, dominates the vast country to the north. I parked, uncomfortably close to the yawning abyss that stretched away before me, set the brake very hard, and stepped out into a fierce cold wind.

Sunset Rock, as is the way of such things, has been painted, repainted, repainted, repainted... Yellow peace signs made up the most recent coat, mostly obscuring the somebody-loves-somebody daubs of the preceding one. The view from the Rock out over Green River Cove to the gray cliffs at Chimney Rock and on to Craggy and Mitchell and Pisgah in the far distance fully justifies the trek it takes to get there. Down to my left Green River Cove narrows like an arrowhead to a point where the mountains to the north meet White Oak's lower slopes. The actual river that gives the wild area its name wasn't visible from where I stood.

From Sunset Rock a foot trail to the west follows White Oak's crest for half a mile up to 3251-foot-high Tryon Peak, which once marked a corner of the border that separated Cherokee land from white man's land.

I continued eastward from Sunset Rock on the road that had brought me up the mountain. The narrow ridgetop of White Oak's western end soon flattened to a surprisingly broad plateau where four small man-made lakes form a chain through a landscaped shallow mountaintop valley just back from the mountain's southern edge. A row of about sixty new condominiums, stacked three deep, is there. The condo windows are the beacons I had seen from I-26.

I stopped and got out to take in the panorama and to say hello to a man standing at the railing. I found that he was staying for a week in one of the condos, having come up from his home in Columbia. He never got tired of the view, he said.

"On clear nights you can even see the Charlotte airport." He pointed east.

Actually, I'm not sure that on that bright morning I didn't see the Atlantic Ocean, maybe even Bermuda and England. It's that kind of view.

From the condos, White Oak Mountain Road, paved from here on, proceeds down the mountain, passes close to the foot of thin, splashy Shunkawauken Falls that I had seen from below, and finally intersects Houston Road at the mountain's foot. A right turn on Houston brought me back to NC 108 and Columbus.

It was noon and, climbing steep mountains being hungry work, I was ready for lunch. Where to eat? No problem. A right turn on NC 108 would bring me quickly to an array of fast food places at I-26. I turned left.

A block beyond Polk County's 150-year-old courthouse, on a wide avenue with angled parking, I came to Rena's

Restaurant, which features home cooking. There I joined other diners who ranged in age from about three to ninety-three and in dress from farmer to lawyer. I had country-style steak and all that goes with it—my kind of hamburgers. At the cash register I bought for 25 cents the latest issue of *THE TRYON DAILY BULLETIN*, which serves Columbus as well as Tryon, and which on its masthead claims to be: *"THE WORLD'S SMALLEST DAILY NEWSPAPER, FOUNDED IN 1928"*.

My edition of the paper contained 52 pages of local stories and ads, so "smallest" obviously doesn't mean "shortest." That claim derives from the page size, which is only that of a sheet of typing paper. Over blueberry pie I read my copy. One article told of "Housecows raised in Landrum". Another informed me who the Red Fox Ladies Bridge Club winners were, while another talked of the area's last Christmas tree farm "boughing-out". The paper was interesting. It took me two cups of coffee to finish it.

In many parts of our country a mountain like White Oak would be a major tourist attraction touted for hundreds of miles in all directions. Here in the Carolinas, surrounded as we are by nature's wonders in such abundance, White Oak is just another mountain. But it's well worth climbing.

# What Color Is The Green River?

THE BRIDGE ON I-26 WHERE IT crosses the Green River two miles north of Saluda has always been a little scary to me. This was so even before the announcement a few years ago that the underpinnings of the eastbound lane were cracked and unsafe (since repaired). Another unnerving fact is that people periodically choose the Green River bridge as their final goodbye place. They climb over the railing and fall 225 feet to the rocks below. Scary.

The bridge is so high that from the driver's seat I can't see the river. For years I have tried, unsuccessfully, to catch even a glimpse of water as I drove over the bridge. I can see that the tree-lined gorge beneath me narrows to a slit at the bottom but I can't see a stream. Maybe the Green River is really just a little creek. Maybe it's all a myth. I decided one winter day to find out.

I left I-26 at Saluda and turned east. Just beyond the Interstate exit Green River Cove Road—narrow, paved, innocuous-looking—branches to the left. I turned onto it.

A sign told me that parking in the road is illegal. Why would anyone want to park there? Another sign says 15% grade. I approached the first hairpin curve. A quick glance down the hill to my right showed seven other roads below me. *Seven*. I realized they were my own road as it switches back and forth down the mountain face. Suddenly I wanted to stop. I knew why people parked. They were afraid to go on. But if I didn't go on down I'd have to back up....

I didn't count all the hairpins on the way down, but eventually came to the valley floor. Before me was the Green River, a broad swift stream tearing along toward the east. No myth. The river water on that day did look green. If we were in copper country I'd suspect pollution, but that's not the case. The river had passed through deep Lake Summit not far above the bridge. Maybe the water's color is from plant life in the lake.

Did the color really give the river its name? I could find no confirmation in the library. Maybe one Zebediah Green was the first settler to see it, and *he* named it. I would like to know.

The pavement ends at the bottom of the mountain. From there a well-maintained gravel road follows the river eastward. I did not see even a footpath leading upstream, westward, into the gorge proper, though I suspect that there must be one of sorts. Many people canoe, kayak or raft downstream from where the river exits the gorge. I have never heard of anyone boating down *through* the raging canyon, but it's probably just a matter of time.

Downstream I saw occasional vacation homes and camping trailers on the river banks, all deserted in winter, but saw no people. Parking places designated for hunters have been cut in the woods on the right of the road. The country is North Carolina game land. The valley—"cove" in mountainese—is a quarter-mile wide at this point.

Pavement resumed after about six miles of gravel and two river crossings on rusty iron bridges. I began to see well-kept houses with signs of people living in them. A few untended old apple trees and sagging log buildings mark earlier homesteads. The valley widened. Four unconcerned deer crossed the road right in front of my car. A mile further a dozen or so others grazed on the far edge of a meadow. I saw none with antlers.

Glimpses through the trees to the right showed the steep slopes of White Oak Mountain, the southern wall of the cove. To the left, beyond the river, rock cliffs tower like monstrous medieval city walls. A jutting point of rock, Wildcat Spur, breaks the line of the cliff. The bald dome of Sugarloaf Mountain can be seen in the background. Green River Cove Road ends at its intersection with Silver Creek Road.

I turned right on Silver Creek, crossed the river again at the head of Duke Power Company's beautiful Lake Adger, then bore right through pasture land and woods to Route 9, where I turned east, toward South Carolina. My river, still green, parallels the highway on the left. The Lake Adger dam and powerhouse are just off the highway to the right at Sunny View Community.

After about five miles on Route 9, at the town of Mill Spring, I turned onto NC 108 and drove along the south side of White Oak through Columbus to I-26. After climbing up through Howard Gap on the Interstate I completed my ramble-circle by recrossing the scary Green River bridge. I still couldn't see water in the gorge below me, but I know it's there, and I know it's green.

# Pearson's Falls—Misty Glen And A Mountain Rescue

I'M NOT SURE WHAT A "GLEN" is. Perhaps real glens occur only in Scotland and Ireland. But one summer day, in a hidden fold in the mountains filled with ferns, green mossy rocks, fresh clean smells, the rush of a mountain stream and the songs of many birds I'm pretty sure I saw a leprechaun. Leprechauns live in glens, so...

Well, if you insist, maybe it *was* a rabbit that I saw jump behind a rock, not one of the little people. Maybe I didn't see an Irish elf, but there is no question of my having seen a mountain rescue.

Even experienced mountain hikers—or perhaps better said, *especially* experienced hikers—must have concern for what would happen if they fell on a wilderness trail. Let's say that far from anywhere you have slipped on some rocks and broken a few bones. You can't continue. Your companion (we will be charitable and say that you were not hiking alone) goes for help. You lie there and wonder.

Who will respond? Will anybody? How many *hours* will it take for help to arrive in this lonely place, even after word is gotten to them? And even if someone does eventually come, how will they ever get my poor battered body down out of the woods?

On old Highway 176 between Tryon and Saluda, about three miles below Saluda, I came one summer day to a side road and a sign that read: PEARSON'S FALLS, ONE MILE. An arrow pointed to the right. You understand, I'm sure, that a dedicated rambler has no choice at such a sign. Without hesitation I turned in the direction of the arrow.

Two minutes on a paved road through thick woods brought me to another sign that said I had arrived at Pearson's Falls. Two cars were in a parking lot to the left, both with out-of-state tags. I parked beside them and went to a nearby little building that houses an unexpected ticket booth. I stopped there, paid a small fee, picked up a brochure and learned from the knowledgeable attendant the history and current situation of the Falls.

I found that the area takes its name from a certain engineer, Captain Charles William Pearson, who found it early this century while scouting a possible route for the proposed railroad from Tryon to Saluda. (The track, which happily did not go through Pearson's glen, was eventually laid and today claims to be the steepest grade of any standard gauge in the United States, rising 600 feet in three miles.)

Captain Pearson was so impressed by the beauty of the area that he bought the land containing the waterfall, settled there, and lived there until his death. In 1931, in order to save the land from lumbering operations, the falls were sold by the Captain's son to the Tryon Garden Club. They built the trail up Colt Creek to the 90-foot cataract, opened the little valley to visitors and have maintained it—leprechauns and all—since.

From the gatehouse I made my way slowly up the trail along the creek. All around me grew a well-behaved jungle of ferns, mosses, orchids, trilliums and other glen-loving plants that give the area its reputation as a botanist's dream. I had learned from my brochure that over a year some 12,000 visitors come to Pearson's Falls, many just to see the plants.

Without warning two of those visitors, a young man and a young woman, came hurtling down the path toward me, the man leading. They were literally leaping over rocks as they ran. Neither responded to my greeting.

Maybe they were in a cross-country race, I thought. Maybe I would meet other runners. I met no one else, however, until, five minutes later, on reaching the waterfall, I found two women and a man standing beside an elderly man who lay unconscious on the wet path. I was told that he had fallen on the rocks. The two cross-country leapers were going for help.

Although I saw nothing I could do to aid the man on the ground, I decided to wait for the arrival of rescuers. Perhaps I could help carry a stretcher or something. As I was going over in my mind the things my waiting there in the woods the rest of the day would cause me to miss, the first rescuers arrived. Barely *ten minutes* had passed since I had met the runners going for help. Two young men, breathless, reached us, nodded, and knelt beside the man on the ground. Both used walkie-talkies or whatever they are now called to pass information to others on the way. Two minutes later three more rescuers arrived with a stretcher.

Since I could offer no help and was just in the way on the narrow trail, I left the group and started back down to the parking lot. On the way I met *nine* other responders to the call for help. They came in three groups, men and women, uniformed and in plain clothes, each with a walkie-talkie. There were four emergency vehicles at the trail entrance, each flashing its red lights. As I drove out of the parking lot a moment later an ambulance, also with flashing red lights, was turning in.

I don't know the rest of the story. Did the fall victim survive? I don't know. But I do know that the speed with which rescuers arrived seemed almost incredible, and that the number who answered the call for help—fourteen people that I saw, not counting those in the ambulance—certainly speaks well of the emergency response groups in the area.

So... if you plan to hike the mountains and expect to break a leg, take someone with you to go for help. If the response at Pearson's Falls is typical—and I imagine it is—help will not be long coming.

# Apples And Apples And The Big Hungry River

AFTER MY DESCENT INTO GREEN River Cove I wanted to know what was beyond those towering ramparts that form the Cove's northern wall. My map showed a considerable roadless area there, between the Green River and Hendersonville, through which several twisty streams pass. One of the streams is labeled "Big Hungry River". I can't read a name like that and not wonder at its origin. I asked a native of Henderson County, my friend Ed Hollifield, about it.

"Big Hungry?" he said. "You want to see Big Hungry? You sure you do? Well, come on. I'll show you. I was *raised* on Big Hungry. I'll show you some apple trees too."

So on a shivery February morning I climbed into Ed's gray pickup, content to let somebody else do the driving for a change. We drove from Etowah to the I-26 intersection and turned south, took the Upward Road exit just below Hendersonville, turned east and entered apple country. Or maybe "apple world" expresses it better.

Orchards, as neat as lawns, begin within a mile of the Interstate. We passed fields of trees of all ages: tiny ones, just set out, their trunks still wrapped in white plastic; half-grown adolescents; mature producers; arthritic oldsters past their prime. We wandered for miles, often on side roads and back ways in the area between Dana and Edneyville, never out of sight of orchards.

(On the day after our excursion I made a followup visit to the library—an integral part of any true ramble—where I learned some apple facts. Did you know that sixteen thousand acres of apples grow in Henderson County? It is the seventh largest among apple-producing counties in the country. In 1988 there were 388 orchards, which produced 65% of North Carolina's apple crop.)

We saw apple packing houses, winter-dormant now like the trees, every mile or so. Small mountains of wooden apple boxes stood, waiting for next September, beside the packing houses. Great bomb-shaped sprayers and heavy tractors were parked behind farm houses. The trees in most of the orchards were already pruned.

An apple tree, you realize, is not just another tree. In May its blossoms inspire love songs; in early autumn its sagging, loaded limbs evoke Thanksgiving and turkey and crisp days. Johnny Appleseed is part of our heritage. And don't forget, it wasn't an orange or a kumquat that Eve nibbled.

In spring, summer and fall an apple tree is a thing of beauty; in winter it shows its strength. The thick ridged trunk and gnarled gray arms of a mature tree, pruned down to hard essentials, speak of toughness and work. Compare a pruned tree with a tangled overgrown unpruned one and you will get a feeling for just how much work that single tree requires. Then think of whole orchards, neat rows and columns of pruned trees marching over entire hills.

The apple country that we had been wandering through is a broad rolling plateau. Plateaus have sides and edges. Near Dana, on King Road, we reached an edge.

"Okay," Ed said, slowing down for an intersection. "You want to see Big Hungry? All right, look."

He turned left onto unpaved Big Hungry Road and we soon entered a steep-sided gorge, heavily timbered, that leads sharply down toward the Big Hungry River and the wilderness beyond. Few people live in Big Hungry these days. Most of the area, like Green River Cove, is now North Carolina game land. That wasn't the case a generation or so ago.

"I used to plow that hill," Ed said, pointing to a hardwood-covered slope so steep I would have had to pull myself up hand over hand to reach the top. "Had to use a hillside plow."

He explained that a hillside plow was constructed on a slant. You plowed one way to the end of a row, then flipped the plow over to reverse the slant, and plowed back. Like a one-sided cow in a steep pasture.

Fifty years ago many people lived in Big Hungry. It was a community. Ed pointed out where once the church, the school house, relatives' farms had been, but it was hard for me to bring peopled pictures to my mind from the thick woods that surrounded us.

Two miles down Big Hungry Road from the plateau we reached the bridge over Big Hungry River, a roaring, crashing, clear mountain creek. Upstream from the bridge are the remains of a dam, a leftover from an early project to draw power from the falling water. On the day of our visit icicles hung on the hemlock-shaded north slope beyond the bridge.

After it crosses the river Big Hungry Road continues through the game land for three more miles then, after fording a small creek, continues on up a hill before ending, according to Ed, a mile or so further. We stopped at the ford and got out.

"My grandparent's cabin was there." Ed pointed to a clearing on the other side of the creek. "Grandmother lived to be 100, had fourteen children. She was a skilled weaver. They always had a garden. The soil was very rich then. On Sundays the whole family—children, grandchildren and great grandchildren, all of us—would get together at the cabin. The children would play in the woods."

A very old cherry tree still grows at the edge of the clearing, the only thing that Ed recognized from that earlier time. He could find no signs of the cabin. Shotgun shells and cigarette stubs on the ground show that hunters now use the area. We stood for a long time beside the whispering creek in the winter stillness and listened.

I could *almost* hear shouts and squeals of children playing, the sounds of another age, of an age not so very long ago by the calendar—only two generations. That age is gone now. Forever, I think.

The next day I tried to find a history of Big Hungry in the Henderson County Library but, except for a few brief mentions, was unsuccessful. I am sure that every cove in every valley in Western North Carolina has a history. They couldn't all be recorded. Pity.

# Caesar's Head...Or Hound Dog's Nose?

You have to climb down through the Devil's Kitchen to get a good view of the stony face that juts out from the mountain's side and overlooks South Carolina. But if you do, there he is, noble Roman nose, thoughtful brow, manly chin — Julius, the greatest Caesar of them all. Or maybe it's Augustus, or Nero. Or maybe...

My parents honeymooned at the Caesar's Head Lodge over sixty years ago. I remember as a young boy seeing snapshots taken there and hearing about what a fine place it was. I decided to go to Caesar's Head, have lunch at the lodge, and perhaps seek out the very honeymoon cabin I saw in my parents' photos. Would things have changed much in sixty years?

Caesar's Head is just across the state line on US 276, in South Carolina, seventeen miles south of Brevard. On a steamy early August morning I drove from my home in Etowah to Brevard on US 64. At the Transylvania County Courthouse with its lush flower beds, I turned left onto US 276. Brilliant white thunderheads had already begun to bulge up over the mountains to the south.

Across the French Broad River, swift and narrow this close to its source, the land begins to rise. Several miles further, on the right, Connestee Falls development begins. With elaborate guarded gates at each end it stretches for miles. I passed the expensive golf communities of Sherwood Forest and Whiskey Creek then the Cedar Mountain Post Office. The "Fox 'n' Berry — Curiosities" shop is on the left just beyond the post office. It looks interesting. Shall I stop? Not today. Today's ramble actually has an objective.

Five miles beyond Cedar Mountain I reached Caesar's Head State Park on the right. Just beyond the park entrance US 276 takes its desperate plunge down the mountain wall into South Carolina. I turned in at the park and stopped at the little gift shop and snack bar there. Since my rambler's principles positively forbid me to ask directions until I'm utterly lost, I set out on foot to find the Lodge, taking a path that leads from the parking lot out to an observation point of bare rocks somewhere above Julius's nose.

An iron railing is there, which is good. I held on tight. As always, on the southern edge of our mountain world, where cliffs fall away to the Piedmont, the view is...well, "awesome," though much overused, is probably the most apt word. From Caesar's Head vast forests stretch out in the direction of the Atlantic. Table Rock rises to the right like a monster granite mushroom. On the day of my visit a cool breeze blew up over the lip of the cliff. Sunlight sparkled with the brilliance that altitude gives it. The tops of the thunderheads away to my right had reached the stratosphere by now and were flattening out, white anvils.

Behind the observation point a sign directs down a hole in the rock to the "Devil's Kitchen." I stepped in the hole, crept down two flights of wooden stairs and entered a spooky crevice, a passage between dripping rock slabs. The path was so narrow I had to move crabwise to get through. The high vertical walls make the passage as dark as a cave, but the floor is smooth.

I traversed the Kitchen, scrambled down a bit of rough path to where a good view of Julius can be had. I stared hard, blinked a few times to make sure my eyes were clear, and stared again. A nose, surely, maybe even Roman, but otherwise the resemblance to Caesar is...well, not overwhelming.

But I had come, not to see a nose, but to find a honeymoon cottage. Anyway, it was lunchtime and I was hungry. Maybe it was even time to surrender and ask directions. I climbed back up out of the Kitchen and went to the snack bar. The blonde young woman at the lunch counter smiled but looked blank when I asked where the lodge was.

"I know it's here *somewhere*," I said. "My parents spent their honeymoon there."

The girl called an older woman out from the kitchen. I repeated my question. She gave me a keen look.

"Why, law me," she said. "There used to be something like that up here, but it burned down *years* ago. I don't even know where it was."

So much for the permanence of temporal things.

Chastened and sobered but still hungry I ordered a ham sandwich and coffee and picked up some park literature, which was a mistake. My faith was about to be shaken again. Not only is the lodge barely a memory now, I learned that even Julius himself is in doubt.

I read that while the generally accepted version of the origin of the name "Caesar's Head" is the resemblance of the rocky profile to that noble conqueror of Gaul, another version has it that the rock was named in honor of a local hunter's favorite hound dog, Caesar, who one day chased a rabbit — his last rabbit — over the cliff.

Anyway, noble Caesar or hound dog's nose, the view alone makes a visit to Caesar's Head well worthwhile.

# Over The River And Through The Woods — The Pisgah Forest Exercise Trail

Hiking in the mountains is often a challenge, sometimes a thrill, always rewarding. But there are times when what you want to do is *walk*, not hike. You can always go to the mall and circle the fountain with your fellow health-seekers, of course. Or you can pace the sidewalks of the town, or maneuver around your house twelve times. You can even, if desperate, walk around and around the car in your garage. Or, if none of that overwhelms you, you can go to Pisgah National Forest near Brevard and take the exercise trail through the woods.

My wife and I walk it most weekends throughout the year. We know every tripping root and slick spot along the way, and can tell you with some precision which wildflowers (not identified by *name*, you understand, but by appearance) you might see at different times of the year. The Davidson River has become a familiar friend. Would you like to go there this morning and take a woods walk?

Yes? Well, come on then, let's go. It's a clear, soft April day. We can look for lady slippers along the river, and see what the trout fisherman are catching. Bring a snack.

We'll park at the Pisgah Forest Ranger Station on US 276, about a mile into the forest from the intersection of highways 191, 64 and 276, about three miles east of Brevard. The exercise trail passes right by the ranger station. Today, as usual, there are a number of cars in the lot, about half with out-of-state tags. A group of hardy, helmeted bikers—the pedaling kind—all decked out in bright helmets, appear to be getting ready to proceed, probably up toward the Parkway.

Ready to start? Don't forget your hiking stick, and your watch. You can be the walk-timer today. Let's aim for 35 minutes for the mile-and-a-half circuit. That's probably fast enough to cause the heart to thump a little but still give us time for a quick sniff of the violets as we pass.

Shall we start to the right or to the left on the trail? It doesn't matter, either way we will wind up back here. Okay, we'll go left.

The trail near the ranger station is flat and smooth, wide enough in most places for two to walk abreast. We come shortly to where the Andy Cove Nature Trail branches to the right. From other walks I know that it climbs the hillside, crosses a gully on a trembly suspension bridge, and then winds through the woods for .6 miles before merging again with the exercise trail a little further on. We will save Andy Cove for another day.

Spring is the best time for wildflowers. Shall we count species as we walk?

"Okay," you say. "What are those little purple ones? Look, they're everywhere. What species are they?"

"I don't know."

"How about those tall yellow ones over there?"

"I don't know."

"What about the little white daisies?"

"I don't know."

"Why didn't you bring the wildflower book?"

"Keep walking."

After winding a comfortable half-mile the trail curves to the left and brings us to the highway. Take care as you cross it. The traffic tends to zoom on this straight stretch of the road. On the other side of the pavement we step around a car barrier and cross the Davidson River on a substantial bridge. Sparkling swift water stretches some distance in both directions from the bridge.

The river level is low today. Protruding wet rocks and ledges cause the many little waterfalls and rapids which give rise to the never-ending rushing whisper of the stream. Three trout fishermen in waders stand motionless beside pools on the upstream side, fly rods extended over the water. I wonder what they hope to catch. The water is not really deep anywhere along here, I doubt that fish of any size could live on this stretch. The anglers probably use fishing as their excuse just for being here in the woods. They'll probably be happy to catch anything big enough to be legal.

Beyond the bridge the trail turns left and follows the river bank downstream. We come to a low, light brown stucco building beside the trail. A small steeple tells us that it must be a church. A sign reads: "The English Chapel, American Methodist, founded 1860." The hours of Sunday morning services are posted. I imagine that many of today's congregations, at least in summer, are campers. Who do you suppose sang the old hymns and filled the collection plate back in 1860?

I want to stop and look around, but you remind me of our trail time target. We proceed.

The path, wide near the chapel, pinches to get through an array of boulders a short distance downstream. An open field spreads out to the right. The unmistakable aroma of campfire smoke reaches us. Campsites can be glimpsed through the trees, we hear children's voices. Here come the first other trail-walkers that we've met today, two young women. A quick "Hi," brief eye contact and they are gone. The path, flat, sticks to the river's edge. Watch out for roots.

"Look, there's a dandelion. Is it a wildflower?"

"Sure, it's in the woods, isn't it? How many different kinds have we seen so far?"

"Eighteen. But you've only identified three."

"Don't quibble."

We complete the three-quarter-mile trek down the west bank of the Davidson and reach another bridge. Several fishermen stand in knee-deep water nearby, others observe them from the bridge. A young man on the bridge holding a long fly rod catches my eye. I look again. Hanging from his belt are two trout, pink-striped rainbow beauties. The fish reach almost to the ground! Ten pounds apiece? Fifteen? More? So much for my thoughts of little fingerlings that the fishermen hope to catch. The water must be deeper than it looks.

I have a fly rod at home, not used for a decade or more. Do you suppose if I got it out and... No, my river-wading days are past.

Across the bridge we turn back upstream, recross the busy highway, wind through more flowered woods to the ranger station and our car. You glance at your watch.

"How long?" I ask.

"Thirty-nine minutes. You wasted time looking at the boy's fish."

"How many wildflower kinds did we count?"

"Twenty-six. Next time bring the wildflower book. And walk a little faster."

The exercise trail—like so many outdoor treasures in our part of the mountains—should be better known. Walking beside the Davidson sure beats mall-striding, at least for me.

# Chatting With Trees At Holmes State Forest

As a general rule, trees seldom make good conversationalists, and the ones at a place I know in Henderson County are no exception. Oh, they are knowledgeable and polite, but tend to be rather one-dimensional in their thinking. They happily tell you all about themselves, but not once do they ask about you and your family, or even talk about the weather. Perhaps they don't care. Would you like to meet them?

It's a bright early fall day, the goldenrod is yellow, the sky blue, the air crisp. Maybe you can get Ms. Black Birch and her buddies to broaden their interests a little and discuss something other than wood. I'll bring sandwiches. We'll have a picnic.

What's that? Oh, don't worry. Don't be afraid. The trees won't hurt you. They may be big and rough, but they can't run very fast.

A sign by Highway 64, at its intersection with Crab Creek Road about halfway between Hendersonville and Brevard, directs to Holmes Educational State Forest, 5.8 miles away. Turn at the Triangle Stop grocery and Texaco station onto Crab Creek Road. Cross the railroad tracks and the French Broad River, pass Reb Hill blueberry farm, Little River Baptist Church and Dupont Road. A couple of miles further, on the right, is our destination.

Turn in at the forest gateway. A Smokey Bear sign tells us that after last night's rain the fire danger is low. We'll stop by the ranger station for trail maps, brochures and a little history. We learn that Holmes State Forest began back in CCC days as a tree nursery for the mountains, a place where seeds for reforestation were produced.

Signs of those earlier working times remain. Experimental plantings of white pine, walnut and other valuable species, grown now to adulthood, provide shade for strollers. A field of small, shapely evergreens near the ranger station is labeled "Christmas Tree Children". A sign explains that the trees are Fraser firs, raised from seeds taken from well-formed parents at higher elevations. In an example of yesterday's genetic engineering, only those "children" in the planting that develop the best Christmas tree shapes will be allowed to mature and make seed. These in turn will be planted by Christmas tree farmers.

From the ranger station we follow a gravel road through a grassy flat field toward the picnic area. Glimpses of something large and bright yellow show through a line of trees across the meadow. It looks like some kind of monster insect. It has wings! Stop here. Let's go see.

Ah, it *is* an insect, a member of that mechanical species called helicopter. Retired from forest service, the huge yellow dragonfly sits poised on a concrete pad for children to climb around and wonder at. Nearby an old mountaintop fire tower has been re-erected, a relic of earlier forest service days. In the field beyond the helicopter a well-worn volleyball court and two serious-looking horseshoe pits wait for players. A gravel path labeled "The Crab Creek Trail" winds through the sports area.

Only three cars are in the picnic parking lot this morning. The wind, straight out of the north after passage of last night's cold front, bites a little when we step out into it. Before we search for our tall, leafy, talking friends, let's find a table in the sun and have lunch. The trees will wait.

From the parking lot we walk across a little bridge and enter the woods, where the delicious damp, musty tang of autumn forest is heavy in the air. A display in a protective shelter contains a map of the forest. Picnic areas are shown on either side of a grassy meadow that we can see through the trees to our left. The map indicates three natural amphitheaters near the picnic areas. Trails, from .3 to 2.8 miles long, roam through the woods. One leads up the mountain to a group campground. The trails are clearly marked as "Easy," "Moderate," and "Difficult". We see that the group camp, which requires a reservation, can be reached by foot from where we are, or by car from Old CCC Road that borders the Forest on the east.

There are several kinds of trails in the forest. One is labeled the Demonstration Trail, where practices of forestry are explained. Another is the Soil and Water Trail, another the Wildcat Rock Trail. And, yes, there is the Talking Trees Trail. But, lunch first.

The picnic tables are beautifully sited in the hillside woods, with much space between them. Most tables today are in dappled sunlight, with table tops and benches still damp from last night's rain. I wish we had brought coffee instead of iced tea.

After lunch we walk from the picnic area up to a rustic building that houses the forestry center, closed today, and from there, across a wooden bridge to the Talking Trees Trail. It is .4 mile long, of "moderate" difficulty. We are told to allot 30 minutes to walk it. Ready? Let's go.

A short distance from the start we come to our first talker, Mr. Yellow Poplar. At a button touch we learn from him about our surroundings and about the huge straight-trunked yellow poplar giants all around us. A couple of hundred feet further is Ms. Black Birch, who has a pleasant voice. We learn from her of the multiple uses of birch wood and of the flavoring derived from her bark. Then White Oak, Basswood, Bitternut Hickory and, finally, Carolina Silverbell tell their stories. (I was a little disappointed to find that Carolina Silverbell has a rather heavy masculine voice. I had hoped for a tinkly soprano, but I suppose there have to be both Mr. and Mrs. Silverbells in the woods.)

Talking Trees Trail ends at its intersection with Wildcat Rock Trail, which is labeled "difficult". Saving it for another time we return to the forestry center.

The sun is warm now. More people are in the picnic area. We hear the shouts of children and the clang of horseshoes. It's time to go. But let's come back. Next time maybe the trees will be a little more loquacious and answer a few questions. Or at least say "Thank you."

Judging from the often sparsely filled parking lot Holmes State Forest, one of the friendliest parks I've seen, does not appear to be very well-known in our part of the state. And that's a pity.

# Wild River, Blue Cheese And A Big Hole In The Ground— Mountain Rest, S.C.

A CENTURY AND A HALF AGO Stumphouse Mountain in the thinly settled westernmost tip of South Carolina stood squarely in the way of progress. The planned railroad that was to link rich Charleston with Cincinnati and the Mississippi valley could not proceed until the mountain was moved. Or until a mile-long hole was punched through it.

Somehow today it seems hard to believe, but the decision was made to punch. Surveying was done and in 1856 a town, Tunnel Hill, was built at the work site. Some 800 Irish immigrants brought over for the purpose set to work with pick, shovel and black powder on the blue granite that makes up Stumphouse. They labored six days a week, twelve hours a day, eventually reaching a tunneling speed of 200 feet a month. That's about seven feet a day, which works out to be a roaring tenth of an inch per man per day. Blue granite must be hard indeed.

Money shortages stopped everything, however; when the tunnel was half finished, the state legislature just refused to continue funding. Then the Civil War came and put final finish to the entire project. The proposed railroad was abandoned, but the hole in the ground remains. You can explore it today.

Stumphouse Tunnel is in a wooded area on the southern edge of the spread-out community of Mountain Rest, where the "big hole" has been an attraction for visitors for over a century. Today it is a South Carolina State Park. From the park's picnic area you can walk to the tunnel mouth and through it into the heart of Stumphouse, where the temperature is always 50 degrees and the relative humidity 90 percent, conditions, in case you don't know it, that are perfect for aging blue cheese. In the 1950s the dairy department of Clemson University used the tunnel for just that purpose.

Stumphouse Tunnel with its unexpected slice of history makes a visit to Mountain Rest worthwhile, but it's far from the little town's only attraction. Remember the movie, "Deliverance"? The stupendous river scenes of the movie were made along the Chattooga River, which in Mountain Rest forms the border between South Carolina and Georgia.

The movie, together with the granting of "Wild and Scenic River" federal status to the Chattooga in 1974, brought the stream to the attention of whitewater people all over the world, and today whitewater rafting is big business. A steady summer procession of rafts, usually filled with soaked squealing people, dances and splashes down the stream. Then high-stacked trucks haul the rafts back up to the start.

Many visitors come to Mountain Rest, and a fair number decide to retire around the several clear mountain lakes in the area. New people come, but the community remains what it was, a mix of apple orchards, roadside fruit and cider stands, several general stores, a post office and friendly people. On a chilly November day my wife and I decided to ramble "down the hill" to Mountain Rest and sample the year's cider crop.

We took Highway 64 west to Cashiers then turned left onto Highway 107, one of the US Forest Service's designated "Scenic Byways." Just outside Cashiers we passed through High

Hampton Inn and Golf Club, the summer home a century or so ago of South Carolina's well-known Reconstruction governor, Wade Hampton. From High Hampton the road descends into South Carolina and ends at SC 28 about ten miles above Walhalla. A left turn brought us to the US Forest Service Ranger Station.

If you go to Mountain Rest, stop at the ranger station for directions to Stumphouse Tunnel and a chat about the region. You can read the history of the community in a locally published book on the subject, and can pick up a copy of the local newspaper, *"The Mountain Ear"*, which promises on its masthead:

"The words are short and the news is all good."

You will learn about another of the region's attractions, Isaqueena Falls. The folks at the ranger station will tell you how to get there. They will also tell you that a legend, a story about the beautiful Indian princess, Isaqueena, goes along with the falls. My wife and I heard from several people *about* the legend but, unfortunately, no one remembered exactly what the legend *was*.

One story has it that Isaqueena, after losing her lover, in keeping with honored tradition, leapt over the falls to her death. Another says that she married a white man and moved to Alabama. A third says that she did indeed leap over the falls, but instead of dying, got up and ran all the way to what is now the South Carolina town of Ninety Six. I will leave it as an archeological exercise for the reader to determine the true fate of the fair princess. Perhaps if you were to look under the rocks at the base of the falls for bits of Isaqueena's royal jewelry...

Anyway, after an exhilarating day of tunnel-tramping, rapids-running, waterfall-leaping, legend-proving and cider-sipping in Mountain Rest you might want to sit down and relax. To music. If so, hike—or you might be ready to drive by

41

that time—to where Highway 107 meets Highway 28. Go into Cuzzin's General Store. If it's Saturday night folks will have come there from near and far, bringing their guitar, flute, fiddle, whatever, to Cuzzin's weekly "Music Making" session. Join right in with your own instrument, or just sit and listen.

Mountain Rest is another of those places in the world that, having been there once, you want to return.

And the cider crop that we sampled on our visit was of vintage quality, by the way.

# Wildflowers In The Clouds—
# The Blue Ridge Parkway

FOUR WILD TURKEYS CAME OUT of the brush and trotted sedately in a line across the highway in front of me. I had to brake lightly to keep from hitting the last one. In shape and coloring just like the many wild turkey paintings I've seen, the birds were larger than I would have thought, huge in fact. Without a glance in my direction they entered the woods just north of where the Blue Ridge Parkway crosses the French Broad River and were gone, an auspicious start to my ramble on a hot early August day up into the clouds of Craggy and Mitchell.

When I travel in our mountains I try always to get to where I'm going by means of the Parkway, even if it involves doubling the driving distance. Easy of access from either I-26 or I-40, the Parkway *immediately* lifts you out of the whine and smell and heat of freeway traffic into a land of forests and silence, where wild turkeys and deer live and where wildflowers cover the roadbanks. Drive for just a few minutes on the Parkway, in either direction from Asheville, and you can be in clouds, or above them.

The Blue Ridge Parkway is surely one of the wonders of today's world, but it's so close at hand we sometimes take it for granted. We shouldn't. Did you know that it is mainly to the Great Depression that we owe existence of the road?

Men of vision had for many years talked of an Appalachian Ridge Road, as it was early called. The first concrete proposals for it were voiced as early as 1909. Ironically, the cost of building the road was always too great during rich periods in our country's history. It was only after we collapsed into the Depression that we were able to afford the Parkway.

Franklin Roosevelt supported building a road to connect the Shenandoah Park in Virginia with The Great Smokies Park in North Carolina and Tennessee as a vast public works project, a way to put hungry people to work. Surveying for the Parkway began in 1934, actual construction in 1935. It wasn't until some 60 years later that the last links in the 469-mile chain were forged. Last year it was reported that twenty-five million people used the highway in the sky.

My August ramble began at the Parkway entrance from NC 191 near Asheville. I turned north, saw my wild turkey troop, drove through Biltmore Forest and the rolling French Broad valley for about ten miles, then crossed I-40 and the Swannanoa River. Here the road began to climb. The Folk Art Center with its quilts and pottery appeared on the left. I shifted to second gear and continued up the slope. To the south the ridge of Town Mountain screened most of Asheville from view.

I met bikers whizzing down the mountain and overtook others struggling up. About halfway to Craggy Gardens I entered a cloud. August plunged into gray, drippy November. A moment later sunshine reappeared, August again. The light around me was brighter, sharper than that in the hazy valleys below. Wildflowers along the road and in the gray and rust-colored rocks of the cliffs on the uphill side of the road sparkled in the sun.

I have a book which describes the wildflowers of our region. I often look at the pictures but can never remember many names. Today I wished I knew more. Banks of yellow daisies predominated, some with dark brown eyes, some with green, some with yellow. I recognized the crimson spiky crowns of bee balm, bergamot, with here and there pale lavender versions of the same flower. Brilliant red cardinal flower spears and purple phlox occurred in patches. Joe Pye weed, named, my book tells me, for an Indian doctor, pushed its rusty-rose billows above the other flowers. Many other species grow in a rainbow of colors wherever a gripping place for their roots exists.

I reached the sign that told me I was in Craggy Gardens. "Gardens" evokes things manmade; flower beds, manicured lawns, tree-lined paths. First-time visitors might well ask, "But, where *are* the gardens?"

Well, they are everywhere, but they owe their existence to nature, not to man. The mixed landscape of massed rhododendrons, flower-filled open grassy meadows, jutting gray boulders and twisted old trees that covers the mountaintop would only suffer if we tried to improve it.

November gray suddenly returned. I pulled off the road at the Craggy Pinnacle overlook and watched an endless cold dark cloud pour like a breaking wave over the ridge then sink to the east, evaporating as it fell. With headlights on I continued slowly through the cold mist toward Mount Mitchell.

Two miles further the sun popped out again and the mists became blinding white masses in a blue, blue sky. The forest around me changed abruptly as I approached Mitchell and the rest of the Black Mountains. Dark spruce now dominated, replacing the maples, oak and ash of Craggy's slopes. A surprising number of chestnut trees survive at the very crest of the ridge, shoots from still-living stumps of long dead giants, some with prickly seed pods showing. All are stunted, however, with browning leaves, all I suppose infected with the blight.

Stark gray skeletons of dead spruce, victims of another blight or of acid rain or just old age, reached above a dark green carpet of living spruce. Black sheer rock cliffs, wet from a just-passed cloud, glistened in the sunlight. I met three more resolute, steadily pumping bikers, strung out a hundred feet apart. They didn't look up when I passed. Another cloud consumed me. I parked again. When the sun reappeared I turned around and headed back the way I had come, south, toward Asheville. I soon caught up with the bikers, passed them and headed home.

In summer, descent into the valley after a time on the peaks always depresses me. First I notice the returning heat. Then the haze. Then the smell of exhaust. I leave the Parkway and, gripping the wheel, squeeze into traffic. Fast food places slide by. More traffic, then home again.

I know I couldn't *live* on top of Craggy. I wouldn't want to. Real November comes, for one thing, and the flowers all turn brown. Still, whenever I am able, I turn toward the peaks, to our sky highway, and climb.

# *In Search Of Sandy Mush*

I FIRST SAW THE WORDS "SANDY Mush, N.C." painted on the side of a church activity bus in the parking lot of a South Carolina state park. Could "Sandy Mush" really be a town name? No, I decided, it was probably the name of a club or something. And even if it were actually a place, it would be a swamp in the sand hills or along the coast, far from the mountains where I live.

My next spotting of the name came on election day. There on the tally board behind the TV announcer reporting Buncombe County election returns was "Sandy Mush" in a list of voting precincts, along with each precinct's vote totals. So, not only does Sandy Mush exist and vote, it's practically my neighbor. I decided to locate it on a map, go there and learn the origin of the name. That seemed a valid ramble-reason.

Actually, I don't need a reason, valid or otherwise, being perfectly satisfied to wander aimlessly along whichever road the car happens to find itself on, but my conscience does twinge just a little when my wife asks where I am going and I can come up with *no* target at all. To have the history of an unusual town name to search out adds a certain dignity to the project.

My state highway map showed no "Sandy Mush" in Buncombe County, but my relief map of Western North Carolina with its wrinkle of mountains and valleys did. There it was, a little open circle at the end of a road in a valley not far west of Asheville. I saw that the large mountain beside

Sandy Mush town was labeled Sandy Mush Mountain, and that the creek that runs near the town is Sandy Mush Creek. I would go there the next morning, a Saturday in early April, and learn where the name came from. How would I find out? Simple. I would just ask a native.

I drove west from Asheville on US 29, turned right on NC 63 toward Leicester, continued another ten miles or so then began to look for signs to Sandy Mush. According to my relief map a road branched to the west from NC 63 and led there. Where was the road? After two passes up and down the highway I stopped at my fail-safe information place, a convenience store.

"Where is Sandy Mush?" I asked the middle-aged woman behind the counter.

"I don't know. Somewhere back over that-a-way." She made a sweeping gesture toward the west.

"Maybe you can answer my other question, then. Why is the town named 'Sandy Mush'?"

"I don't know. You can ask the owner, maybe, but she ain't here. She's a native. I only been here eight years. Sorry. Try asking at the Trading Post up the road, why don't you?"

I went to the Trading Post and was told to turn left on Sandy Mush Creek Road, about a mile further on NC 63. No, they didn't know why it was named Sandy Mush.

Sandy Mush Creek Road winds through a narrow valley for several miles, past neat houses on each side of the road. Large herds of black-and-white cattle wandered in pastures that were almost iridescent with the green of April grass on the day of my visit. I crossed a one-lane bridge and reached the foot of a low, steep, wooded hill. The road made a couple of twist-arounds on the way up, but eventually brought me to the crest. Down the other side I passed Hog Eye Road on the left, then emerged from the woods. Before me lay Sandy Mush.

"Shangri-La" was the first thought that came to mind.

Sandy Mush is a giant bowl in the mountains, a soft, tamed, walled garden with walls three thousand feet high. The bowl is cracked on its eastern edge, the crack forming an escape route for Sandy Mush Creek on its way to meet the French Broad. Where Shangri-La had its monastery, Sandy Mush has its churches, Baptist and Methodist, straightforward impressive buildings standing on rises in the floor of the bowl. I saw a large cemetery beside one church that must go back to the time of the early settlers of the region, a time not really very long ago.

The floor of the bowl is rolling green fields interspersed with patches of woods. Large prosperous-looking farmsteads occur at intervals, each with its cattle herd. As I passed one farm two huge white geese were standing beside the road. One hissed at me. Sandy Mush looks like a Constable painting.

My comparison with Shangri-La is inappropriate, though. It's inadequate. A lost valley in the Himalayas, monastery or no monastery, may be beautiful, but it is simply not up in the same league as Sandy Mush and the rest of our Carolina high country.

Fine, but my excuse for coming in the first place was to learn the origin of the region's name. So, find a native to ask. The only business that I saw in the valley was Darlene's Country Store, all by itself in the center of the bowl. I stopped there and topped off my gas tank. An old man, as tough and worn-looking as the mountains that loomed over us, was alone in the store. I asked if he would mind answering a question.

"No sir," he said. "What you want to know?"

"Where did the name 'Sandy Mush' come from?"

"Durned if I know. Any other questions?"

I decided then that the name's origin is simply lost in mountain mists or washed away by the creek. Nobody knows.

Or cares. But *I* care, so *I'll* tell you what Sandy Mush means. It's the white man's best attempt to anglicize an Indian word, "Hsangdeemughtqs", which means "Land of the She-Bear That Growls at Full Moon." How do I know that?

Durned if I know. Any other questions?

There, end of story. No, not quite. As so often happens, I took one step too many. I went to the library. After considerable searching, I found this: A group of early hunters in the region stopped beside a creek and made supper. They cooked mush for their repast and used unsettled creek water in the cooking. Their mush turned out to be sandy, so... Actually, I like my version better.

But, however it got its name, Sandy Mush is a wonderful place to ramble to.

# *When Warm Springs Turned Hot*

I APPROACHED THE RUINS CARE-
fully, my eyes watching the ground for sharp rocks, snakes,
whatever. On a bare, roofless masonry wall that rose from the
earth before me were markings that appeared to be a form of
writing, an inscription of some kind. I wanted to get close
enough to decipher, if possible, those ancient daubs. I reached
the wall and there, barely discernible through the fading, peel-
ing paint, were these words:

MINERAL BATHS - $1.50
MINERAL WATER - 50 CENTS PER GALLON

The ruins I was looking at are not ancient, just old. In
fact they are not in the strict sense ruins at all. They are what
remains of the resort and health spa at the town of Hot
Springs, North Carolina, thirty miles or so down the French
Broad from Asheville, not far from the Tennessee border. The
"ruins" today are in the process of being rejuvenated.

If the planned resort development in Hot Springs that I
was told about is carried through, you will, after a hiatus of
two decades, once again be able to relax and mend body and
mind in a hot mineral bath. The price of the bath may be
higher than it was when the above sign was painted but the
steaming water will come from the same springs. There will be

a golf course in the new resort. A helicopter landing site is being prepared and there will be other attractions, but the center of focus will still be the springs.

Until white settlers came to the French Broad valley in the late 1700s, Indians had long used the hot spring waters for healing. Soon after Europeans settled the region a health spa was built. The town that grew up around it, at that time called Warm Springs, became a popular summer resort. In 1831 a hotel that could accommodate 250 guests was opened to serve summer visitors and travelers on the first road across the mountains that could be called such, the Buncombe Turnpike, which followed the course of the French Broad and passed through Warm Springs.

In 1886 the name of the town was upgraded from Warm Springs to Hot Springs. I could find no record of the spring water having increased in temperature at that time, so I suppose the town fathers must have decided that if you weren't a *cold* spring then you should be a *hot* one, not just a warm one. Hot Springs maintained its popularity for many years, but the coming of the railroad foretold prosperity's end.

When the tracks eventually crossed the mountains, the old Buncombe Turnpike quickly fell into disuse. Instead of being on the main east-west road as it had been for so long, Hot Springs suddenly found itself on a seldom used byway. People gradually stopped coming and the Hot Springs Resort faded away, closing completely twenty years ago and falling into the ruins that I saw. The passing of the resort left behind a pretty mountain town hoping for a return of past glories. With the current renovation of the springs, more than just hope is in the air.

Hot Springs today is a clean, uncrowded village on a flat point of land at the confluence of the French Broad River and Spring Creek. A freshly painted red Southern Railway caboose sits in a small park in the middle of town and serves as visitor center. A ranger station for Pisgah National Forest is next door to the caboose. Several river-rafting companies have located along the French Broad there, and wilderness outfitters take advantage of the proximity of the Appalachian Trail.

Hot Springs, even in the temporary absence of mineral baths, is geared for the summer visitor and is a pleasant place to go to, well worth my afternoon's ramble.

# Poetry And Trees—
# Joyce Kilmer Memorial Forest

T RY TO IMAGINE WHAT THE LAND we live on was like before the white man came, before the forests were cut. Writings by early travelers like William Bartram help, but at best our vision of the way it was is dim and misty. But you don't have to imagine. You can go to a place in far western North Carolina and see for yourself. The place is called Joyce Kilmer Memorial Forest.

Joyce Kilmer was born in New Brunswick, New Jersey in 1884. As a student at Rutgers he wrote a short poem inspired by an old oak tree that grew on the Rutgers campus. He titled the poem "Trees." Is there anyone, any adult at least, who is not familiar with it?

In 1918 in France, on a front-line mission for which he had volunteered, Sergeant Kilmer was killed by a German machine gun bullet. His body lies now near where he died, in a grave in some woods near a village called Seringes. He left behind a wife and five children. After the war "Trees" was translated into many languages. Somehow the simple little poem came to be, throughout the world, a symbol of the horror that mankind had just passed through.

In 1934 veterans of Kilmer's army unit, the 165th Infantry, Rainbow Division, proposed a memorial to him, and asked the US Forest Service to select an appropriate place for it. After a lengthy search throughout the country the Forest Service finally settled on a site in North Carolina as the most fitting place for a memorial to the author of "Trees." On a sunny June morning I went there and walked the silent paths of that memorial. We are fortunate that it exists at all.

In the first decades of this century, before creation of the national parks and national forests with the protection and control they provide the land, the forests of Western North Carolina were cut down. An incredible amount of prime timber was removed from the mountains. Very little was spared the axe and saw, but an isolated area of Graham County must have been too rugged for profitable timbering even with the rip, slash and drag methods of 1910. For whatever the reason, the land was not cut over and large plots of virgin forest remain today. Almost four thousand acres of these woods-as-they-were make up the Joyce Kilmer Memorial Forest.

Dedication of the memorial occurred on a rainy day in the summer of 1936. Several dignitaries missed the ceremony; they were stuck in the mud some miles from the site. Kilmer forest was not chosen because of its easy access for man. It was chosen for its trees.

The memorial is about a two-and-a-half-hour drive from Asheville. To get there you go west on I-40, turn onto US 19 at Waynesville, climb through Balsam gap, pass Bryson City and the head of Fontana lake, climb up Nantahala Gorge beside the river with its endless summertime stream of rafts, kayaks and canoes as colorful as a flock of water butterflies, then bear right on Highway 129 to Robbinsville. In Robbinsville turn left and follow signs. Ten miles on a paved road brings you to Joyce Kilmer Forest. Leave your car at the picnic area on the banks of Little Santeetlah Creek and walk into the woods to the head of the trails.

An open shelter shows a trail map. Faded photographs of trail scenes hang on the shelter walls together with a copy of Kilmer's original handwritten "Trees." From the shelter several miles of well-maintained trails lead up into the forest.

The first objective of a trail-walker is usually the Kilmer Memorial itself, a bronze plaque set in a boulder in a grove of massive hemlocks about a half mile into the woods. From there the trail loops up the hill for another mile before winding down again to end back at the picnic area. The trees you walk through on all the trails, though not as big as California's redwoods, evoke the same sensations as their western cousins.

Poplar, hemlock, oak, ash, sycamore, beech, basswood, some trunks over 150 feet tall and eight feet in diameter, fill the forest and form a leafy ceiling high above. Some of the trees are said to be five hundred years old. Little light and little sound penetrate the forest. Footsteps on the spongy brown path are silent. Speech echoes as in a cave, hollow, resonating; you tend to whisper. Bright green moss covers the jackstraw tangle of ancient fallen giants that forms the forest floor. Gray dead trunks rise here and there among the living trees, split at some time in the past by lightning, or just finally succumbed to old age.

Snails, slugs, orange salamanders and black and yellow centipedes live in the rotting trunks of the forest floor. New trees sprout from the crumbling old logs. The air is cool and moist. Water drips from rocks.

I was pleased to see not even one tiny bit of trash on the trail, not one initial carved in a trunk. And this is after more than a half century of public use. I am certain that if young Sergeant Kilmer could walk today in his forest, among his trees, he would be pleased.

After the passing of eight decades since the lumbermen came through, woods again cover the slopes of the Great Smokies, the Blue Ridge, the Cowees, the Snowbirds and all the other Carolina mountain ranges. But they are not the forests of the past, not yet, not for centuries to come.

I recommend you go to Kilmer Forest, follow the trails, look up, be still, listen. Try to imagine how our mountain world looked back in the days when only the Cherokee walked the land. Maybe it will look that way again some day. For our distant descendants.

# Balsam Lake—Jewel Of Pinhook Valley

NOT LONG AGO MY NEWSPAPER noted that the Balsam Lake Recreation Area of Pisgah National Forest had won an award for its handicap-friendly design. Having seen on an earlier ramble a sign pointing west from NC 215 toward Balsam Lake, I set out on an afternoon in late August to find the lake and see for myself why it won an award. The sun was bright, the sky blue and white, and the breeze warm. *Any* excuse for a mountain ramble on a day like that being good enough, out came my maps.

From Etowah I drove west on US 64, through Brevard, then nine miles further to where the North Fork of the French Broad meets the main stream. Turning right onto NC 215, I entered the area known as Balsam Valley. With car windows down to catch the late summer scents as well as sights I drove as slowly up the valley as the sparse traffic would allow. The road goes beside the swift North Fork, crossing it several times.

On the day of my ramble the roadside banks were brilliant with the colors of the estival season, that time of year when, growth finished, most plants just relax, make flowers, smile and enjoy the shortening days that tell of the approach of fall and winter. The leaves of many low shrubs were already bright red. Goldenrod and several kinds of yellow daisies grew in clumps. Rusty-rose puffs of ten-foot Joe Pye weed, often with pale yellow tiger swallowtail butterflies perched on them, reached above most roadside growth. Dark purple asters and pink phlox were scattered here and there. I smelled distinct whiffs of autumn in the air.

About five miles up the valley a sign welcomed me to Balsam Grove Community, which stretches like a string for several miles along the river. I noticed, as I have on other late summer mountain rambles, neat rows of blooming dahlias in a rainbow of colors in many roadside yards. Beyond Balsam Grove Post Office and Calloway's Restaurant are the ponds and sluices of Headwaters Trout Farm, which features a gilded trout on its signs.

At the upper end of Balsam Grove the land rises steeply and the road begins to twist its way up toward the Blue Ridge Parkway. High up to the right on the crest of the ridge I caught glimpses of the gray prominence called Devil's Courthouse, a favorite trial ground for that hardy breed, rock climbers.

Fifteen miles up the valley from US 64 (two miles down from the Parkway if I had come from the other direction) I reached a gravel road that led to the left. Two signs there invited me to turn. One sign read PINHOOK VALLEY and advertised a campground, the other, BALSAM LAKE RECREATION AREA AND LODGE. There was no indication how *far* I would have to go to reach either place.

I turned left and proceeded at a pace appropriate to the unpretentious gravel way, expecting on rounding each curve to see the glimmer of a lake ahead of me. I drove past homesteads built around substantial old mountain cabins, past Pinhook Valley Baptist Church, past Christmas trees by the tens or hundreds of thousands marching in neat rows and columns across whole mountains, past Charley's

Creek Baptist Church, through dark evergreen groves, across racing brooks. The scenery was beautiful, but nowhere did I see a lake.

Finally, after creeping along for five miles at fifteen miles an hour—which on an unfamiliar back road seems not a drive but a journey—I reached my goal, Balsam Lake, a sparkling body of water lined with black-green balsam trees.

Mine was the only car in the parking area near a picnic shed at the head of the lake. A log bridge and trail sign beckoned. Three yellow swallowtails and one black cousin rested on the sign. The trail, which runs at water's edge along the steep side of the lake for a half mile from the headwaters toward the dam, was clearly one of the reasons for Balsam Lake's handicap-friendly award. For most of its way the trail is flat and smooth, ready for wheelchairs. Several solid wooden platforms extend into the lake from the trail. Signs tell that the lake is trout water, that it is supplied by a hatchery and that there are no lure restrictions for fishing.

Bullfrogs that sounded like hippos started a chorus around me. I saw black shiny salamanders on the trail and huge tadpoles in the shallows. A belted kingfisher flew out from the brush ahead of me. I stopped and listened. The only sounds were the garumphs of frogs and wind in the balsams.

I walked to the dam. Across the lake I saw the lodge, a large bungalow built on a level spot up from the water. An elaborate dock and fishing platform, the wood of its recent construction still bright, juts over the water below the lodge. I retraced my steps around the lake. A lady was fishing from shore near the bridge at the headwaters. She had caught five trout, she said, including a "real nice one."

I left the parking lot and drove on up the road to the lodge, but the driveway to it was blocked by a closed gate. A sign read RESERVATIONS ONLY. Not having brought my fishing tackle with me I left the lake with its lucky fisherwoman and headed toward home.

The five-mile drive back through Pinhook Valley, familiar now, seemed almost too short. At NC 215 I turned left, uphill, to the Parkway then drove north, past Devil's Courthouse, the Graveyard Fields and Looking Glass Mountain. Where US 276 intersects the Parkway I turned right, toward Brevard, and descended through the Pink Beds, by the Cradle of Forestry and Looking Glass Falls, to the Brevard Ranger Station. There I learned that Balsam Lake Lodge, which has five bedrooms, can be reserved by groups. Information on rates, etc. can be had by calling the Pisgah National Forest office, (704) 586-2471.

When I got home to Etowah I realized I had driven some three hours to get to and from my destination, but had spent only one hour there.

Was it worth it? You bet.

# Carl Sandburg's Home

A TOUR OF CONNEMARA, CARL Sandburg's home for the last 22 years of his life, is a journey back in time—but not so very far back. On the one hand the house is a museum, like Mount Vernon is a museum for George Washington. On the other hand, a visit to Connemara is stopping over at a neighbor's place for a chat. Or maybe just to borrow a cup of goat's milk.

At least it's that way for someone who, like me, lived in Carl Sandburg's time. For baby boomers and their thoroughly modern offspring Connemara is probably a fascinating glimpse of prehistory, of a harsh, testing, microwave-less, computer-less age.

"But how did he *write*? What did he use for a word processor?"

I have been through Connemara several times, escorted on each visit by an enthusiastic and knowledgeable guide. Careful to stay within permitted lanes, never touching the furniture or knick-knacks, I just look and listen.

The first thing that comes to my mind on thinking about those visits is a small detail, a copy of Life Magazine, open, just as Sandburg left it, on a cluttered desk. The magazine seems so natural, so un-historic. I believe I even recall the actual article displayed. The second thing that comes to mind is the poet's library. Books—fiction and nonfiction—are everywhere. They fill shelves, stand on tables and desks, rest beside beds.

According to the guide, Sandburg had not just read them all, but was familiar with the contents of each. They were his indispensable reference library, the Internet access of his day, I suppose.

I have friends who knew Carl Sandburg. They remember him as that "old man who always needed a haircut" often encountered on Main Street in Hendersonville. I don't think his being a famous poet made much of an impression on his neighbors at the time.

But then I imagine there must have been people in Virginia a century and a half ago who remembered having seen, and not been particularly impressed by, ex-president George Washington—who probably needed a haircut too—strolling the streets of Alexandria after his retirement from America-fathering. But with the passing of years there would have come a point when no one then alive had seen the living George. He would stop being a man and become a legend, just as Mount Vernon changed from being a farmhouse to a museum of ancient history. So it will be for Carl Sandburg and Connemara in our lifetime.

The Sandburg home is in Flat Rock, North Carolina, three miles south of Hendersonville on US 25. If you drive there from Hendersonville, you will pass historic Saint John's in the Wilderness Church on your right, then the Flat Rock Playhouse. At the old Flat Rock post office—now a shop called the "Book Exchange"—turn right onto Little River Road. The entrance to the Carl Sandburg Home National Historic Site is on your left. Park in the lot and take the short path down to the visitor center for maps and background.

You will be able to see Connemara from there, on a hill across a pretty lake. Take the shaded quarter-mile path up the hill to the house or use the phone at the visitor center to call for transportation if you prefer. When you reach the house I suggest that, before taking the formal inside tour, you wander around the well-maintained grounds a while. That will give your mind a chance to reorient itself to life as it was a generation or two ago. Perhaps you will want to stroll back to the barn and start your visit there.

If you do, be sure to introduce yourself to the gentle descendants of Mrs. Sandburg's champion goats that you will find in the barnyard. Maybe sit on a bench there and chat with them a few minutes about modern farm life. Then go and look into the springhouse, the chickenhouse and other necessary outbuildings of a farm from the past, but keep in mind that the "past" is just thirty or forty years ago, not long-gone pioneer days.

You might take time to hike one of the several trails that lead up Glassy Mountain from the house and barn. If you do, note carefully the signs that tell you to watch out for poison ivy and snakes. Realize that the snakes, like the goats, are probably also descendants of farm residents from Sandburg's time.

After your hike, relaxed and fully oriented, go back to the front of the big white house and join a tour. They start in the room below the main house entrance, running every half hour from 9 a.m. to 5 p.m., and cost $2 for an adult. Watch a well-done film about the poet, then follow your guide through book-crammed rooms, the kitchen, the laundry and work spaces. Take time to read book titles and magazine subjects as you pass.

Try to picture the house alive, working. Listen to the silence demanded by the poet when he was writing. Hear the clatter of pots and pans in the kitchen and the rumble of the early washing machine downstairs. Hear doors slam, people call. If you are old enough, imagining life as it was then won't be hard to do.

When you finish the tour go back to the small gift shop in the basement. Buy some post cards if you like, but be sure to select a book of Sandburg's poems. And don't just buy the book. Take it home and read it. Try reading some poems out loud. Read them more than once.

Imagine that Sandburg—the old man who needed a haircut—is reading them to you. Let him be sitting on your bench out by the barn, maybe strumming his guitar. If you are lucky he will intersperse his poems with songs.

Go to Connemara and get to know Carl Sandburg, before it all becomes ancient history.

# The Expensive View From Highlands

THE REAL ESTATE BUYER'S Guide that I picked up on Main Street in Highlands, North Carolina got right to the point: "The view alone is well worth the asking price of $787,500." Presumably the well-sited house has golf privileges as well as view since emerald-green courses snake through the woods and valleys in and around Highlands. Ah, that view...

Actually, on the November morning of my visit, fog and misty rain obscured everything further away than about fifty feet. Fog has its good points, though. It helped on the drive up and down the mountain on US 64 that connects Highlands with the French Broad Valley near Rosman. I wasn't able to see the thousand foot drops a couple of feet from my tires that day, so was able to relax, imagine that the sun was shining and enjoy the scenery. The views of Whiteside Mountain and all of the high country around Highlands, on a clear day, *are* magnificent, even priceless.

So the asking price for that house with the view was really a *bargain*.

On my Highlands visit rain may have mostly obscured the mountains but I could see Main Street. There were four lines of parallel parking, two down the center of the wide street and another at each curb, and all places taken. And this on a rainy weekday in November, well past leaf season. I had to cruise up and down several times in the cold drizzle before I found an empty slot. Some of the cars were from North Carolina, a scattering from Tennessee, Georgia and South Carolina, but the majority were from Florida. Big cars. Sleek. Worthy of Highlands' views.

My wife and I strolled in the rain up one side of Main Street and down the other, dropping in at several of the warm, bright shops along the way. Three times I heard Floridians commenting to store clerks on the cold weather, and asking if it was going to snow. One Florida couple in the Old Edward Inn where we had a delicious lunch asked the server to have their table moved out of a draft. I suppose for someone who lives in perpetual warmth, flatness and sunshine, a trip to the high mountains in November offers challenge, a hint of hardship, a pinch of danger. They should try it when glaze ice is on the roads.

The tone of Highlands is set by the shops. No "tourist junk" is to be found. Art galleries alternate with boutiques, along with a scattering of interesting restaurants. Most businesses were open on the day of our visit though a few had closed for the winter. I managed to fend off the boutiques but enjoyed several gallery-wanders. I like to look at paintings done by local residents, at sidewalk shows and such. In my experience *all* such paintings, though they might be interesting and appealing, look amateurish. I try to see just what it is about them that says to me, "local artist." Few offerings in Highlands have that look.

One mountain landscape that I rather liked, for instance, had two notices taped to its frame: "DO NOT TOUCH PAINTINGS" and "Price-$5000". One gallery holds an auction every evening at 7:30. About a hundred comfortable chairs are lined up before the auctioneer's stand. Museum-quality Chinese carvings, antique furniture and rolled oriental rugs line the room. If you attend the auction, bring your checkbook. Highlands is that sort of town.

How did it get that way? When did it start? Unlike most towns, which evolved over time from small beginnings, Highlands was deliberately created.

In 1875 a certain Captain S.T. Kelsey came from Kansas to the North Carolina mountains to "plant a town." He bought land in Macon County and on it built roads and erected buildings, then advertised his four-thousand-foot-high town as a resort. I suppose he also named it, though I don't know. In any event outsiders, mostly rich families from Charleston and the South Carolina low country, read Captain Kelsey's ads, probably during the first July hot spell, and came to Highlands. They and other flatlanders have been coming back ever since.

My wife and I enjoyed our brief visit to the town and plan to return next spring when we can see the view. We'll visit the Nature Museum, explore Dry Falls and try out the lines of rocking chairs on the sidewalks outside several inns. I imagine even with the crowds that must come in season, Highlands will cope nicely. Everyone we talked with was friendly and helpful. And not all of the paintings cost $5000.

I'm sure the good Captain Kelsey would be pleased today with the way the mountain town he planted back in 1875 has sprouted and grown.

# Old Fort—Mountain Gateway

ARE YOU BOTHERED ON RAW winter days by a cold or perhaps a little case of consumption? Drink cocklebur tea. Do you have impure blood? Drink burdock tea. Suffer from chills? Just catch a frog and hold it until it dies.

These are some of the remedies our pioneer forefathers used, or at least that is what visitors to the Mountain Gateway Museum in Old Fort are told. You can also cure your warts by stealing someone's dishrag and hiding it.

Today's Old Fort is a descendant of the little pioneer settlement that guarded America's wild western frontier—and I don't mean the wild west of Texas or Montana. I mean the earlier, older wild west of the time when the eastern slopes of the Blue Ridge Mountains were literally the country's frontier. The British had declared that the land beyond the eastern edge of the mountains belonged to the Cherokees. It was off limits to white settlers, another country. Pioneers might stand and gaze at the forests across the border, but by law could not possess them.

Of course pioneer families looked and, British and Cherokee wishes to the contrary notwithstanding, moved in, cut trees, built cabins and plowed the soil. Trouble soon followed. Indians raided outlying farms. People were killed. Not surprisingly the Cherokees sided with the King when, after the Declaration of Independence, war with Britain threatened.

The people of North Carolina soon decided that the Cherokee enemy at their backs would not do. Early in the war, in 1776, General Griffith Rutherford with 2500 Carolina men undertook to end the threat and to solve the "Cherokee problem" generally. To solve, that is, the problems that the whites who had settled Cherokee lands were having. The problems of the Cherokees with the encroaching whites were just pushed another step along the ugly, rocky path that was to lead before many years to the Trail of Tears, the banishment of the Cherokee nation to the *new* wild west, Oklahoma.

Before Rutherford took his expedition into Cherokee country he assigned five hundred men to build a fort to support his invasion. The place he chose was near the headwaters of the Catawba River, at the foot of the mountains, below Swannanoa Gap. When fort construction was well underway he led his army up through the gap, into the French Broad valley and beyond.

There he destroyed thirty-six Indian towns and, more important, that year's corn harvest. In the campaign there was little loss of life; the Indians fled at the soldiers' approach. A year later, in 1777, the Cherokees ceded large tracts of mountain land to the colonists. Rutherford's fort was no longer needed. In time it vanished. Not even it's exact site is known today, but the town that started as a frontier village around it remains, Old Fort, Mountain Gateway, proud of its pioneer heritage. Go there and learn a chapter from our mountain past, of our nation's story. The place to start is Old Fort's Mountain Gateway Museum.

The museum, located in the middle of the town beside rushing Mill Creek at the probable site of Rutherford's fort, is housed in a building constructed by the WPA sixty years ago. Two authentic mountain pioneer homes, the Morgan and

Stepp cabins, have been brought to the site and reconstructed beside the museum.

One of the many activities associated with the museum is Log Cabin Meals. On certain days during the year lunches and dinners of traditional mountain food are prepared and served by women of local churches in the Morgan cabin. In winter the cabin is warmed by a crackling fire in a huge rough stone fireplace. Information about Log Cabin Meals and other museum affairs can be gotten by calling the museum at (704) 668-9259.

Inside the museum building artifacts and pictures complement a fifteen-minute film that tells the history of the region, often through personal reminiscences of older residents. Construction of the first railway into the mountains, a nine-mile convolution of curves and switchbacks that covered the two-mile distance between Old Fort and Swannanoa Gap, is featured in the film and in a number of photographs. An assortment of home remedies such as the ones noted above is displayed. There is no admission charge for the museum.

From Old Fort you should venture out into some of the mountain country you just learned about. Don't even consider just turning around and taking I-40 back home. Explore. Go away from the Interstate, up the coves that lead off from the valley roads, to where things aren't really so far removed from pioneer days. You can go south, east or north from Old Fort, or more or less in these directions. There are few straight roads in the region. (You can also go west from Old Fort, of course, but that will mean getting back on I-40 and into the zoom and swoosh of the twenty-first century. Put that off as long as you can.)

If you choose to go south, you will pass through Sugar Hill Community, named not because sugar was made there but because a wagonload of sugar hauled laboriously from

Charleston tipped over and spilled there. Continue beyond Sugar Hill. At the intersection turn right onto US 64, pass beside Lake Lure and Chimney Rock, climb up through Chestnut Gorge to the apple orchards of Edneyville and continue on to Hendersonville.

If you prefer to go north from Old Fort, take US 70 east, turn left onto NC 80 at Pleasant Garden Community, then climb up past Lake Tahoma to where NC 80 crosses the Blue Ridge Parkway. If the weather is good turn left on the Parkway and drive past Mount Mitchell and magnificent Craggy, then on down to Asheville.

To see the mountains east of Old Fort, take US 70 to NC 226 just out of Marion, then climb up to Little Switzerland where it perches on the crest of the ridge at the Parkway. Stop at North Carolina's Minerals Museum then...

But you have your own maps. You decide where to go. There is hardly any direction you can take, any road you can drive on, that won't lead you into mountain country settled by tough, tenacious people who followed Rutherford's expedition into the lands beyond the western frontier, beyond the fort, through the Mountain Gateway.

# A Busy Day In Loafer's Glory

SEVERAL SUMMERS AGO CHARLES Kuralt and company presented their famous "North Carolina is My Home" show at the Brevard Music Center in a benefit performance for the Hendersonville Symphony Orchestra. One of the pieces in the show is a long recitation of the names of Tar Heel towns, from Why-Not to Samarcand to Molly to Spot, etc. Of one particular town Mr. Kuralt said: "And then there's 'Loafer's Glory.' Oh how I'd love to know *that* story." I decided when I heard him that I would search out Loafer's Glory and learn its story for him.

On an earlier ramble through Mitchell County I had seen a sign pointing to Loafer's Glory, so I knew its general direction. One late summer morning I set out, planning to spend the day strolling the streets and looking at the various sights of the town. Perhaps I'd find a rocking chair on a porch in the shade. I'd take along a knife and a stick to whittle. In short, I would go to Loafer's Glory and...well, loaf.

I climbed onto the the Blue Ridge Parkway at its intersection with NC 191 near Asheville and drove north, past Craggy and Mitchell, to the intersection of NC 80, and turned left. After a plunge down the upper slopes I passed through Busick and Celo, made a zig right on US 19 at Micaville and then a zag left on NC 80. After ten twisty miles down the Toe River valley NC 80 ends at its intersection with NC 226. A left turn, another mile, and I reached the outskirts of my destination.

Perhaps I should stop here and say that if you decide to go to Loafer's Glory, don't plan to spend the whole day there. What I found, you see, is that the outskirts of the town *is* the town, whose most prominent feature is the green-and-white LOAFER'S GLORY highway sign that says you're there. I parked on the edge of the road and got out. Just beyond the highway sign, on the left, is the General Store.

Ah, that's what I was looking for. Here would surely be a row of dedicated, porch-rocking, stick-whittling, chaw-chomping mountain loafers. If there were an empty chair I'd join them.

Alas, no more. All of that has been swept away, by the rush, hustle and flit of today, I suppose. The General Store, though it retains its sign, is now a fabric shop and sewing machine repair center. There are no loafers, no rocking chairs, not even a front porch. There's only a small parking area situated, I imagine, for the benefit of visitors like me who want to photograph the store's historic sign.

Across the highway from the fabric shop is the rest of Loafer's Glory, a long low building that houses a beauty shop and Bonny and Clyde's Snack Shop. That's all there is. Several trucks were parked beside the snack shop. I went in, ordered a soft drink and asked the busy young woman behind the counter where the town's name came from. (I'm sure I am the very first person in history ever to ask that acute, penetrating question.)

She wasn't sure. "They say some man a long time ago named it. Maybe."

I left Loafer's Glory, drove through Bakersville and Spruce Pine and from there back up onto the Parkway. After a quick stop at Little Switzerland for a huge ice cream cone I headed for Asheville, not quite managing to keep ahead of the butter almond's drip as I drove.

On the way home I had an unexpected bonus. Somewhere on the north side of Mount Mitchell I saw beside the Parkway a wildcat. It was about three times the size of a house cat, with a tawny, mottled coat, small ears, long legs and a short tail. After giving me a cool, level stare it faded unhurried into the woods. Beautiful animal. I hope to see it again.

I'd had an interesting ramble through magnificent country, but had failed utterly in my mission to learn the story of Loafer's Glory. I adjourned to the library, where after considerable searching in the North Carolina history room I found that the town was named about 1890 by one Jonathan Burleson in response to the habit of the town's men of whiling away time on the porch of the general store. (I was right in my mental picture, just a century late.) Fine, that was a start. Now, who was Jonathan Burleson and why was it up to him to name towns?

No success. In neither thick, dusty genealogical tomes nor histories of the Toe Valley region and Mitchell County did I even find Mr. Burleson's name mentioned.

I don't think I'll bother Mr. Kuralt with what I learned.

On a proper ramble you should never know just what you're going to find. Sometimes there's not much "there" when you arrive. Which is just as it should be. It's the "I wonder..." that makes rambling so much fun.

On my map, not far from Loafer's Glory, is the metropolis of Bandana. I wonder...

# In Grandfather's Shadow—
# Banner Elk

To reach Banner Elk from Asheville you take highway 19E and drive to Minneapolis. Minneapolis, North Carolina, that is. Minneapolis is just on the other side of Plumtree and this side of Cranberry.

All three towns sit on the banks of the North Toe River, so named, according to the library, for an Indian girl, Estatoe, whose lover was killed by her kinsman. However the river got its name, the Toe is a beautiful high valley stream. As you drive beside it watch out for trout fisherman with their wispy fly rods and hip boots. One is likely to come struggling up out from the roadside brush anywhere along the river. On a hot hazy day in mid-August I drove up the Toe valley, through Plumtree, Minneapolis and Cranberry, then over the ridge into the Elk River valley, on my way to the town of Banner Elk.

Why?

Need I have a reason? I suppose so. Well, for one thing, I had never been to Banner Elk. It lies in the center of what had been a blank spot on my mental map of North Carolina. That's a sufficiency of reason, I think. And of course I wanted to know how Banner Elk got it's impressive name, though it seemed obvious. I pictured the scene.

In days long gone a great elk, "Wapiti" to the Indians, a veritable giant of its kind, lived in the valley of the small river that would someday bear its name. One morning an early settler of the region, hunting with his musket in the cool valley mists, saw the noble animal and killed it. Later, at a local fair of some sort, the hunter displayed the mounted head of his elk and won a prize, a banner.

Not so, says the library, which gives this pallid explanation: Prominent among the early settlers to the region was the Banner family. In all, seven Banner brothers, who were of Welsh descent, came to the Elk valley. The town that grew up around the Banner homesteads became known as Banner Elk. Not very exciting. Maybe I should stop going to the library.

The country changes abruptly when you cross from the Toe valley into the Elk valley. The Toe flows through a land of typical mountain homesteads, many not so far removed from hard-scrabble times. They stand on steep slopes beside vegetable gardens and sagging outbuildings, usually with one or two deceased vehicles growing in the weeds somewhere in the yard. "Tatertown Road" branches off to the left. (I *must* look for Tatertown someday.) Signs tell that the highway along the Toe is the "Overmountain Victory Trail," the route taken by John Sevier and his men on their way to defeat the British at Kings Mountain more than two centuries ago.

On the day that I drove along the Toe, masses of perfect dahlias in every color you could imagine (except, I think, blue) grew in beds before many homes. At one place an old man in overalls was just entering a patch of tall corn with a basket in his hand. On each cornstalk I could see two brown-silked ears ready for pulling. Toe valley is real mountain country, stable and settled. But not rich.

It all changes when you cross the ridge and approach Banner Elk. Before you reach the town you pass a long asphalt airstrip that parallels the highway on your right. On the hills beyond the airstrip are chalets, new Swiss-looking homes sited for their view, not for nearness to water as were the homesteads on the Toe. At Banner Elk's 3700-foot elevation, the air, even in hot August, was crisp. North Carolina's latest recorded killing frost occurred there some years ago, on June 1.

A few miles beyond the airstrip, in Banner Elk center, many businesses have a fresh-painted, spruce look and sport names like the "Corner Cafe and Cooking Company", "Alpine Ski Center" and "Edge of the World Outfitters". Most have fancy carved wooden signs in bright colors, often with gilded letters. Directions for skiers to places like Beech Mountain, Sugar Mountain Resort and the like are everywhere. The town—or perhaps better, village—is home of Lees-McRae College.

I decided that Banner Elk is a place I want to return to, perhaps even in winter. Or maybe in October for the annual Woolly Worm Festival, where the official prognosticator for the coming cold season is selected in a no-nonsense, winner-take-all worm-crawl race up a string. What the woolly worm predicts is important, since Banner Elk and surroundings is ski country, waiting for winter and praying for snow (of which it gets about 50 inches annually).

On Sugar Mountain and in other scenic sites outside Banner Elk town, condominiums rise like mushrooms. One huge condominium complex, a shocking great rectangular pile of a building, perches—like a Rhine castle without turrets—atop a mountain to the east of town. In the condo country around Banner Elk elaborate manned gates in manicured settings guard developments hidden in the woods out of sight of the highway. Community "Crime Watch" signs occur at close intervals.

Grandfather Mountain, with its oldest-in-the-world rocks and mile-high bridge, looms over everything a few miles to the east of Banner Elk. Over the past billion or so years

Grandfather must have watched many things happen in the valley at his feet. He's probably wondering now what will happen next. He's probably laughing.

I returned to Asheville by way of the Blue Ridge Parkway, entering where it crosses a corner of Grandfather. On the way home I stopped off at Little Switzerland again and bought an ice cream cone, three large dips of vanilla. Soon Mount Mitchell loomed across the valley to my right. Then Craggy. Then down the hill to Asheville. I had colored in the blank spot on my map and learned some history.

But I still see in my mind great Wapiti standing, head high, in the cool river mists.

# The Vance Birthplace

It has been said that at the turn of the century in North Carolina more sons, dogs, horses and mules were named Zeb than any other name. This was done in tribute to Zebulon Baird Vance, a mountain man who rose up during Civil War times to lead North Carolina through its hardest years.

Zeb Vance was many things. He was a unionist turned Confederate soldier, three times governor of North Carolina, US senator. He was a man who chewed tobacco, told frequent jokes that made the ladies blush, and packed Senate galleries when he spoke. He could also laugh at himself.

The Vance Birthplace in the Reems Creek valley north of Asheville, literally in the shadow of Craggy Peak, is preserved as a state historic site. A visit to the Vance Birthplace will take you back to the days, little more than two lifetimes ago, when Reems Creek valley was frontier, to an era when you grew or made what you needed or you did without. It was a time when old soldiers who had fought in the Revolutionary War and remembered King's Mountain and Cowpens still lived. The visit takes you back also to the Civil War, to the wrenching times before, during and after the fighting, to harsh years that cried out for strong leaders, for men like Zeb Vance.

On a cold bright late winter day I visited Reems Creek valley and the Vance Birthplace, descending to it from the high mountains that form the valley's eastern wall. To get there I took the Blue Ridge Parkway from its intersection with US 70 east of Asheville and drove north almost to Craggy Gardens, to where a paved road branches to the left. A sign at the intersection directs to the Vance site.

Away from the almost level Parkway the road abruptly collapses and slides down the north slope, still winter-bare on the day of my visit. A cold front had passed through during the night and snow-covered Craggy Peak to my right gleamed like the Matterhorn in the March sun. Coming down from high mountains is in some ways like starting long ago and moving forward in time, from yesterday with its homesteads hacked from the wilderness to today's split-level houses, monster green tractors and three-cars-in-the-driveway.

After leaving the high ridge you always come to the first house of the valley below. Or, perhaps better said, you come to the *last* house of the valley, the one above which no one, not even the hardiest settler in desperate search of land of his own, ever felt that living was feasible. These days often abandoned, crumbling and in the process of returning to forest, this highest homestead is always situated near the pinched narrow top of a fold in the mountain beside a small swift stream.

As you descend further you also move forward in time. The little stream of the first homestead gets bigger and the houses you pass progressively more prosperous until you reach the valley floor with its lush, level fields and well-kept homes—today.

On the day of my ramble the winter pastures were greening, and maples along the creeks were red with flowers. A few yellow daffodils bloomed in protected places. Where the road down from the mountaintop intersects Reems Creek Road a sign directs right, toward the Vance Birthplace site, a mile further.

On the site, the original Vance log cabin and six outbuildings have been reconstructed. The cabin is built around the original chimneys and is furnished as it was in Vance's time. Little imagination is required to see there how life was lived 150 years ago on the frontier.

A visitor center with a museum is near the parking lot. The museum, concerned with Vance and his family, focuses on the Civil War period. His sword and pistol and other mementoes of the time are displayed, as is a wooden bathtub from the Vance cabin. Many photos and paintings catalog the life of Vance and his illustrious family. You learn that Zeb's grandfather fought in the Revolution at Kings Mountain, that his father was an officer in the War of 1812, and that his brother was a Confederate general and later a US congressman. The story of Vance's early life is told.

When young Zeb's father died, his mother moved to Asheville where her seven children could get an education. By age twenty-five Zebulon had become coeditor of the *ASHEVILLE SPECTATOR*. From 1858 to 1861 he served in the US Congress. In the turmoil leading up to the Civil War he opposed secession, but when Lincoln called for two regiments from North Carolina to fight her sister states, Vance said:

"I died last night a Union man. I am resurrected today a secession man."

He fought as a Confederate officer at New Bern and Malvern Hill. Then, in 1862, without having campaigned, he was elected governor and spent the rest of the war "fighting the Yankees and fussing with the Confederacy." Because of his earlier unionist sentiment Vance was not trusted by Jefferson Davis, a fact that Vance felt contributed to weak defense of eastern North Carolina by the Confederates and its fall early in the war.

During Vance's three terms as governor he was an advocate of universal education. In his second term women were first hired as teachers. He was elected to the US Senate in 1879, serving until his death at age 63 in 1893.

Zeb Vance is not ancient history. A few people alive in the mountains today were born when he was their senator. A visit, a slow thoughtful one, to the Vance Birthplace can make a lot of history real.

# Roan Mountain—Canadian Island In North Carolina

Several years ago my wife and I climbed Craggy Peak at the height of rhododendron bloom. We found a young woman, a park ranger, stationed at the very tip-top of the mountain to answer questions from the steady stream of visitors emerging from the pink tunnel that was the quarter mile trail up from the parking lot. The ranger agreed with us that the flower display on Craggy was almost unbelievable, but then she added that Craggy, of course, didn't compare with Roan Mountain. I had never been to Roan Mountain but decided then and there to go.

On a foggy, drizzly morning in early September I undertook to find out what's so special about "The Roan," as it's called. I could have wished for better weather, but had resolved long ago never to postpone a fishing trip—or a ramble—because the sun wasn't shining. By ten o'clock the rain stopped, the clouds parted and the rest of the day was all chamber of commerce.

From Asheville I drove north to Mars Hill, continued on US 19 a mile or so past Burnsville then turned left on NC 197, past Green Mountain to Red Hill. (I think there's a Blue Knob and a Big Yellow Mountain in the area too) A right turn there brought me to to Bakersville. It's all good road, not too twisty.

I had not realized how big a crop tobacco is in that area of the mountains. Many small tobacco fields, most of them wedged along creek bottoms in narrow valleys, had reached the gold-green stage. Some fields had already been harvested. The tobacco leaves had been pulled from the plants and attached to stakes to dry in the sun. The rows and columns of drying leaves in the fields looked like so many little wigwams.

In Bakersville I turned left onto NC 261 and drove up the fourteen miles to Carver Gap on the crest of Roan Mountain, passing a trout farm, Christmas tree plantations and more tobacco on the way. Although the road climbs steadily— Roan Mountain at 6286 feet is only a few pine trees lower than Mount Mitchell—it does not convolute and bite back on itself as much as I had expected.

The Roan, which spreads above and to either side of the route from Bakersville, does not have the rugged wildness of Mitchell and Craggy. It is smoother, rounder, softer-looking. I was surprised to find how high I had actually climbed when I reached the top and looked back.

At the crest, just before you cross the Tennessee line, a road branches to the left toward Roan Mountain Gardens. The peaks that rise on both sides of the highway at the gap are almost treeless expanses of meadow called mountain "balds". A number of cars were in the Carver Gap parking lot, and a straggle of hikers could be seen creeping up and down the slopes to the east.

I followed the sign toward Roan Mountain Gardens. The road, paved most of the way, runs along the crest for several miles, rising steadily. Rhododendron clumps, open grassy areas and stands of dark evergreens cover the mountaintop. Three large parking lots, mostly empty on this "off-season" day, occur at intervals. Well-kept trails, flat here on the smooth dome, lead off from the lots. The foundation of the old

Cloudland Hotel, a 268-room vacation spot that lasted until 1903, is a short distance from the first lot.

Near the end of the park road are the Rhododendron Gardens. Two senior citizen ladies dressed in brown National Park uniforms passed out maps and directions at an information booth at the beginning of the garden trails. On the day of my visit the sun, even at 6000 feet, was hot. One of the ladies was sitting on a rock outside the booth.

"There's so much fog up here," she said. "We take advantage of every bit of sun that comes along."

Trails in the garden are level and paved with asphalt. One is labeled "The Handicapped Trail." They ramble between opaque walls of rhododendron interspersed with patches of meadow and frequent glimpses of endless mountains to the east. A wooden platform built out over the rhododendron lets you count peaks in those mountains if you have the patience.

Promotional literature from the last century claimed that from the Roan 50,000 square miles of country can be seen, with 100 mountaintops over 4000 feet in the view. I didn't count miles or peaks but don't doubt the statement. I was told that on a clear day you can even see the Smokies to the south.

Roan Mountain was discovered by botanists soon after the land was opened by Daniel Boone and other early pioneers. Unusual plants, many of them natives of eastern Canada that were pushed south by the glaciers, are found there. An example is the rare scotch heather which covers many of the meadows. The famous botanist, Dr. Asa Gray, claimed the Roan to be "without doubt, the most beautiful mountain east of the Rockies."

As is often the case, the origin of the mountain's name is a mystery. From the usual assortment of legends—Indian word, type of tree, etc.—I choose to believe the name

89

commemorates a roan horse (whatever that is) left on the mountain by Daniel Boone.

Another mystery mentioned in park literature is the ghostly "mountain music" heard from time to time on the mountain. It is described as sounding like the humming of thousands of bees. The ranger in the booth admitted she had never heard it but assured me it was true, which just gives me another reason to return.

Roan Mountain should definitely be near the top of your Carolina To-Visit list. Maybe you will hear the mountain music. Or even find Daniel Boone's poor lost horse.

**October Sunrise – The French Broad Valley near Holmes State Forest**

**Balsam Lake – Jewel of Pinhook Valley**

**The Thomas Howard monument and plaque**

TO·COMMEMORATE THE BATTLE OF
ROUND MOUNTAIN IN WHICH
**CAPT. THOMAS HOWARD**
AND HIS BRAVE FOLLOWERS
WITH THE FAITHFUL INDIAN GUIDE
SKYUKA. DEFEATED THE CHEROKEE NATION
1776

ORIGINALLY ERECTED BY
TRYON COUNCIL NO. 143 JR. O. U. A.M. 1909

THOMAS HOWARD
FEBRUARY 25, 1760 – FEBRUARY 24, 1838
S. C. MILITIA, ROEBUCK'S REGIMENT, REVOLUTIONARY WAR

RE-ERECTED 1967

**Town Creek Indian Mound**

**Cabin at the Vance birthplace near Asheville**

**Pioneer Days at Old Fort**
Photo Credit: Eileen Johnson

**Wildflowers by the Blue Ridge Parkway**
Photo Credit: Eileen Johnson

**Modern-day patriots fire a volley – the annual reenactment of the Battle of Cowpens**

**Patrick Ferguson's grave at Kings Mountain**

**Lookout Point on Roan Mountain**
Photo Credit: Eileen Johnson

**The Blue Ridge in March – a cold view from the Parkway near Craggy Mountain**

**Caesar's Head....or Hound Dog's Nose?**

**Carl Sandburg's home in Flat Rock, North Carolina**
Photo Credit: Eileen Johnson

**Sliding Rock in Pisgah National Forest near Brevard**
Photo Credit: Eileen Johnson

# Nature's Rollercoaster, Forestry's Cradle, Yard-Long Trout—Climbing Pisgah's Southern Slope

Civilization is, from time to time, a good thing to get away from. In our part of the country there are many escape routes. One easy way to decivilize yourself is to enter Pisgah National Forest near Brevard.

At the intersection of highways 64, 191 and 276, where 276 begins its long wiggly ascent to the crest of the Blue Ridge on its way to Waynesville in the valley beyond, stands a large old stone gate. If you drive through the gate a transformation, abrupt and complete, will occur. Behind you will lie Wal-Mart, traffic, heat, glare and noise, before you only cool, green woods.

Come on, it's a hot July Saturday afternoon, let's go there. I'll show you.

Oh, you're afraid too much woods will bore you? You say that once you've seen one tree you've seen the whole forest? Don't worry. Pisgah National Forest, cool and quiet though it may be, is anything but boring. It's exciting! Like the State Fair at hog-judging time, maybe. Bring your bathing suit. And your courage. Let's go!

US 276 enters Pisgah National Forest through the stone gate and follows the course of the Davidson River for several miles. Sycamore Flats picnic area, the first of many on the way to the mountaintop, comes up shortly on the left. Its half-mile-long paved, flat, one-way road that winds among the picnic tables beside the river is a favorite strolling place for Brevardians throughout the year. Today it looks to be full of picnickers. A whiff of campfire smoke reaches us as we pass.

A mile or so further a road branches to the left and crosses the river. A sign directs to the Davidson River Campground, a very popular camping place that stretches with many loops and twists for more than a mile along the river. In summer it is usually full of tents and camp mobiles of various sorts. In winter the campground's main road is a good place for a brisk hike.

Just beyond the campground turn-off is the ranger station and visitor center on the right of 276, in an open area of lawn and big trees. The parking lot is full today. Let's stop anyway. We can pick up brochures, maps and information, and look at living trout in an aquarium exhibit inside.

From the visitor center the highway hugs the Davidson for several more miles. We come to a sign and a gravel road that tells us that horseback riding is available 1.5 miles to the right. We'll save that for another day. We pass Coon Tree picnic area, also full, on the left. Hip-booted trout fishermen in full angling regalia, most standing by a car or pickup readying fly rods, occur at intervals.

We reach a fork in the road. Here US 276, the right fork, forsakes the Davidson River and continues up the mountain beside Looking Glass Creek. The left fork stays with the Davidson and leads, according to a sign, to the Pisgah Center for Wildlife Education—Fish Hatchery. We bear left.

About a half mile from the fork we pass the start of well-known Looking Glass Rock Trail. I count thirty-six cars in the packed trail parking area and along the nearby roadside. The trail up Looking Glass starts innocently enough in thick woods at the base, but eventually winds up on the scary 4000-foot top of the Rock with its smooth, slippery flats and vertical cliff-sides.

We can stop now and climb if you've had enough woods-looking. Shall we? Oh, you say that cliffs—particularly when you're looking down from the top of them—scare you. Okay, just remember you had the opportunity. I don't want you to be bored. Let's go on to the trout hatchery.

A mile further we turn left, cross the Davidson on a temporary bridge just downstream from the remains of the old bridge washed away in a flood a couple of years ago. I see that construction of a replacement is underway. Beyond the river another steep mountain, John Rock, rises to form the southern wall of the Davidson valley here. Wet areas on John Rock's bare stone cliffs high above us glisten in the sun. I suspect you'll not want to climb John Rock today either, right?

Several fishermen are wading in the river near the bridge as we cross, hoping, I suppose, for escapees from the hatchery. This parking lot is almost full too. It's good to see so many people taking advantage of a beautiful day to enjoy an outing in our woods.

We squeeze into a parking place and stroll among the many nearby trout runs. Rainbows, browns, brooks, ranging in size from tiny minnows to monster breeding stock—to my eyes at least a yard long—live in the different runs. A constant gushing flow of clean cold mountain water from the Davidson maintains ideal growing conditions. Catching-sized trout from here are used to stock streams all over the mountains.

You want to feed the fish? Okay, put a quarter in the little box over there and get some pellets. Now sprinkle them in a run. See the trout practically jump out of the water to grab them. I wonder just how hard it would be to catch one of those beauties when it's been released in a creek.

Finished feeding? Now find a place to wash your hands. Sniff them. They'll smell like fish food.

We leave the hatchery, return to the fork in the road and turn left on US 276. Looking Glass Falls is a short distance ahead, to the right. The Forest Service recently extended the parking area there, but today we still encounter a minor traffic jam. We won't stop, but you can see the falls from the car. It's a good thing that people taking pictures of something doesn't wear that something out. If it did, Looking Glass Falls would by now be just a smooth place in the creek.

Maybe we'll come back here one cold day next January, when the whole area is encrusted with ice and shrouded in mist. The creek level will be winter-high then and the falls will thunder like a freight train. Looking Glass Falls in winter can be almost overwhelming.

I wonder if the Cherokees 500 years ago made treks up here just to look at the falls. I'll bet they did.

Beyond the falls the highway begins to climb seriously. We follow Looking Glass Creek, criss-crossing it several times. Eight miles in from the forest entrance we reach Sliding Rock, nature's original rollercoaster.

We'll turn in and park somewhere. Needless to say, on this hot Saturday even the newly added-to parking lot is crammed. There are a number of buses and large vans, many from churches, some from as far away as Ohio and Mississippi. We'll follow the trail of bathing-suited children to the slide area. Squeals and shrieks ahead tell us we are going in the right direction.

We stand at a railing above the actual rock, a natural, glassy-smooth chute in the gray stone of the stream bed. A line of people—mostly young, but some mothers and fathers escorting little ones—wait at the top of the slide. They shuffle forward until their turn comes, sit down on the brink, let go their hold on the rock, screech, and in a slithering zoom descend toward the pool below. They hit with a resounding splash. Most sliders, dripping and shivering, immediately get back in line to do it again.

I'll bet Cherokee children, centuries before Columbus, did the same thing. I'll bet they screeched too.

You want to slide? No? You're sure? You're not finding the woods too boring, are you? I told you to bring your bathing suit. And your courage. Let's go.

Three miles further up 276 we reach the Cradle of Forestry. I'll turn in and stop at the entrance booth, you get out your wallet. It costs $4 apiece to enter. Steep, yes, but worth it. We'll stay awhile. They have a snack bar that serves barbecue. And a movie. It's dark in the movie, you can snooze if you feel the need. Then we can spend some time in the extensive Forestry Museum. And then we'll hike.

Yes, hike. You'll be all rested and refreshed by then. And, don't worry, there aren't any sliding rocks or cliffs, or even rough spots on the trails.

Two main trails start from the visitor center. Each is about a mile long and easy-walking. We'll take the Forest Festival Trail first. It shows forestry as it was in early logging days and describes the approaches taken by Dr. Carl A. Schenk—the father of forestry in America—to restore and maintain Mr. Vanderbilt's woods. Exhibits along the way include a logging locomotive and a sawmill, together with plantings of different tree species made by Dr. Schenk and his students. At a small pond a ranger even gives fly casting lessons to would-be anglers—probably to people who saw the man-eating trout back at the hatchery and want to catch one.

Back at the visitor center we'll now take the Biltmore Campus Trail, which leads to the one-room cabin that housed Dr. Schenk's actual school and to other little log houses with names like "Black Forest Lodge" and "Little Bohemia" that served as dormitories for his students. Several cabins are furnished as they were then. Demonstrations of pioneer life are given by people dressed in costumes of the day. Today a lady seated at a spinning wheel on the porch of one of the cabins is making wool yarn for our benefit. It's fascinating to watch the process.

Step along, now. Don't lag.

We leave the forestry center, follow twisty 276 on up to the top of the ridge and turn right on the Blue Ridge Parkway. Three miles up the Parkway we reach the ridge-hugging Pisgah Inn. Shall we stop here for another snack? Before we take the *real* mountain trail up to Pisgah Peak, then—

Oh, come on! You can't be *that* tired! You *are*? Okay, but you're not bored, are you?

# Town Creek Indian Mound

CEREMONIAL MOUNDS, TEMples, burial grounds, archeology. The words evoke ancient Egypt or the jungles of Central America, but they also apply to the pine woods of North Carolina.

In Montgomery County, about fifty miles east of Charlotte, between the towns of Mount Gilead and Samarcand, on high land overlooking the Little River where it joins Town Creek, the Peedee Indians five hundred years ago raised a sacred mound. Sixteen feet high with broad steps leading up to a temple on its top, the mound looks like a small version (which it is) of much larger mounds found in the lower Mississippi valley. You can climb the mound today and enter the dark, thatched temple reconstructed there.

Town Creek Indian Mound is one of twenty-four historic sites administered by the North Carolina Department of Cultural Resources. The sites range across the state, from the Thomas Wolfe Memorial in Asheville to the Duke Homestead in Durham to Confederate Fort Fisher in Wilmington. I have visited half the sites. Each is well maintained, with a knowledgeable and interested staff. I intend to see them all. A brochure describing the historic sites is available from North Carolina Department of Cultural Resources, 109 East Jones Street, Raleigh, N.C. 27601.

A visit to a place like Town Creek, where people once lived but live no longer, always raises inevitable questions: Who were they? When did they come? From where? How long did they stay? What did they do here? And finally, what happened to them? The answers to these questions, or as close to answers as we can come, are arrived at through archeology, which for the most part means digging where the people lived.

The first controlled dig at Town Creek was begun in 1936 and is an ongoing project today. The area around the central mound has been meticulously uncovered. Post holes of a stockade surrounding the mound were found by the diggers, as were remains of the temple on the mound's top, a burial hut, a priest's dwelling and a game field. The stockade fence and the three buildings have been reconstructed and a tall pole with a bear's skull at its top erected where it served as the goal in the Peedee's lacrosse-like games. Knowing that the poles used in the reconstruction are actually placed where the original poles stood adds considerably to the realism of the scene for me, as does a representation with life-size models of a funeral preparation in the burial hut.

A slide show in the visitor center tells the story of the Indians of the region before arrival of Europeans, and explains in detail the purpose and activities of the temple and stockade area, which archaeologists say was in use for two centuries— for about as long as America has been free of British rule, to put it into perspective.

The area within the stockade fence was used for ceremonies and tribal gatherings; the only permanent residents are thought to be have been priests. Important tribal leaders were buried there. A number of graves have been located and some excavated. Relics of all kinds are housed in the visitor center.

According to those who have studied the site, the Peedees, a branch of the Creek Indians, arrived at Town Creek around 1450 from the south. They drove out the dwellers of the time and established villages across the area. The stockade around the temple served for defense against raids by the displaced occupants and other invaders. The Indians left no written records, so details of their day-to-day life must be pieced together from the bits and pieces of durable objects—stone and bone and pottery—that accumulated over the passage of some eight generations.

From the meager record that has been left, what we can know is limited, but—right or wrong—archaeologists have reconstructed a surprisingly full account of Town Creek life. We are told, for instance, that the Peedees practiced head-flattening. An infant was bound to a cradle board and a bag of sand fastened to its head until its skull became molded into a permanent backward slant. This was done to increase the beauty and intelligence of the new tribal member. Perhaps it's just as well we don't know *too* much about the old customs.

Around 1650 the Peedee tribe left Town Creek, presumably returning southward from whence they came. Little is known about the cause of the abandonment of their home for two centuries, or of what happened to them after they left. Encroachment by Europeans, a process which in a very short time disrupted irrevocably each of the Indian cultures it touched, probably figured heavily.

Where are the Peedees today? I found one reference, which states that remnants of two tribes, the Cape Fears and the Peedees, were moved in 1715 to South Carolina, where:

"By 1808 these two tribes were represented by a single half-breed woman."

I conclude that, as is the case with many of North Carolina's early dwellers, there probably *are* no Peedees today.

The Town Creek Mound site is located in a beautiful area of managed sandhill pine forests. Plantings of pines ranging from tiny seedlings to ancient giants occupy the land for miles around. On the late winter day of my visit the large grass areas inside and surrounding the stockade had just been mowed; everything was trim and polished in readiness for warm-weather visitors. The site is well worth a visit.

# *Along Rutherford's Trace To Cherokee*

A<small>RCHEOLOGISTS TELL US THAT</small> Indians walked the land we live on for at least ten thousand years before the first Europeans arrived. A hundred centuries, starting with woolly mammoths and carrying forward to a settled time of agriculture. A *hundred* centuries. America in 1976 celebrated its bicentennial, *two* centuries. What will the land look like ninety-eight centuries from now? The *land* will still be here, but...

Enough! Let's go to Cherokee and see how Columbus-and-all-that changed the way of life of those who were first on the land. I've been to Cherokee in summer, milled with the tourists and enjoyed "Unto These Hills," but never in winter. Is the town even open in January? Let's take advantage of this cold, shining day and find out. We'll start early, right after breakfast. Ready? I'll drive this time, you look.

It's a perfect winter morning, with hard frost, still air, no clouds, smoke rising straight up from chimneys. The sun has just peeked over the ridges to the south as we leave Asheville on I-240 west, cross the French Broad, take the US 19 exit west and drive up the Hominy valley toward Canton. A historic marker is ahead on the right. Since I can never read more than about six historic words on one of the signs as I pass it at highway speed I'll pull off and stop. The sign says:

RUTHERFORD TRACE
"The expedition led by Gen. Griffith Rutherford
against the Cherokee, Sept., 1776, camped nearby
along Hominy Creek."

Who was Rutherford? Was he maybe a rambler like us? Had his expedition been sent out to observe how the Cherokees lived in those early days? Did he perhaps want to find ways to improve relations between the red man and his white brother?

Not exactly.

The Cherokees had sided with the British in the Revolutionary War that had just begun and were raising havoc among the settlers all along the frontier that ran through the middle of the Carolinas. Rutherford had been sent, with 2500 soldiers and 1400 pack horses, not to *observe* the Cherokees but to destroy them. He didn't succeed, but he came close.

After building a fort at the base of the mountains below Swannanoa Gap (at today's Old Fort) Rutherford's army climbed the steep slopes up from the piedmont and crossed the French Broad River near today's Asheville. Picture the scene.

Men, horses and pack mules straggled behind for two miles when the head of the column reached the river. Imagine that line of men and animals splashing through the wide, swift stream, with surprise attack from the woods on the opposite shore a real possibility. Now compare that river crossing with our own sixty-mile-an-hour zoom across the bridge.

It took us less than a minute. Could Rutherford's army have managed it in a day? Did they set up camp once across the river to regroup and dry out? Did they have breakfast before resuming their march? I wonder what they ate for breakfast. Something like cold jerky and corn bread, probably. Let's stop at the next McDonald's. I want coffee.

In a monumental understatement, I'll say that things are different today from the way they were in Rutherford's time. About the only things that are the same are the mountains that rise on all sides of us. Pisgah dominates the skyline to the south just as it did for Rutherford, and the "rat" climbed Pisgah's eastern side then as it does now, though in the virgin forests of the time Rutherford probably got few glimpses of it.

One sharp difference between then and now, very noticeable on this still winter morning, is the air we breathe. The reek of paper mill hangs heavy, thickening as we approach Enka, Canton and the Champion International Company. It will dissipate when the sun warms the frost-covered earth and the cold air trapped near the ground rises, but in the early morning of our ramble the distinctive odor is quite strong. Rutherford's air would have held only the scent of pine with maybe some lingering woodsmoke.

Beyond Canton the land rises. The paper mill aura disappears. Tourist-aimed signs telling of the glories of the Great Smokies begin. In the neat valley town of Clyde we pass a store—a trading post?—called "The Old Grouch's Military Supplies." Rutherford probably stopped there for musket balls in 1776.

We leave Rutherford's Trace where it branches to the left toward Waynesville at US 23, thus avoiding passing through the places where the burning, slashing and trampling of the General's campaign took place. Maybe someday, on another ramble, we'll follow his trail to the end.

Continuing peacefully on US 19 toward Cherokee we pass the Methodist's Lake Junaluska Assembly on the right and soon enter the town of Maggie Valley, where several miles of wide Main Street, winter-empty but swept and clean, wait for spring. (Someday I *must* find out who Maggie was.) Shops, restaurants and motels, most of them closed, line both sides of the street. Structures that are part of Ghost Town in the Sky are visible on top of a high, steep mountain to the right. A cog railway near the western end of town carries tourists up the mountain to the restaurants, rides and regularly scheduled gunfights that take place there. It's closed today.

Beyond Maggie Valley things get a little tawdry, with signs that say things like "Indian Blankets, $9.99". US 19 climbs up to Soco Gap where it passes under the Parkway and begins a long, steep, winding drop down into Cherokee. After descending for several miles we reach the narrow, flat valley floor. Small, neat houses and a few pastures with cattle soon give way to the town proper.

I ask you now to ignore Santa's Land, Cherokee Bingo, a shop that sells fake medieval armor, and another which has a befeathered, frozen-looking man beckoning mechanically from a chair by the front door. This section of Cherokee along US 19 is ready and able to handle the *hordes* of tourists that will descend on it come warm weather, but today the street is almost empty. We'll turn right at a sign toward the Museum of the Cherokee Indian.

After a short drive along the picturebook Oconaluftee River we turn left, cross the rushing trout stream and park at the museum. At 9:30 on this January morning ours is the only car in the very large parking lot. Imagine the scene here on a hot July afternoon. See the parking lot crammed. See curious, fake-tomahawk-toting tourists wandering around looking for "real Indians." Now put the scene out of your mind and don't bring it back.

We are the first museum visitors of the day. A young woman at the desk collects the $3.50 admission charge from each of us. The building seems new and in good repair. Inside the museum proper, displays and audiovisual shows trace the Indians' story, from their crossing over the land bridge from Asia ten thousand years ago in pursuit of the hairy elephants of the time, through their subsequent spread across North America. The tribes that developed on this continent are noted, and Cherokee civilization before the white man described. Recordings of many Cherokee legends and myths as told by tribal elders can be heard at the touch of a button. A great many stone arrowheads and other implements are displayed.

We learn the story of Sequoya and his creation in the early 1800s of a Cherokee alphabet, and hear recordings of Cherokee speech with associated printing in English and in Sequoya's script. Sequoya is claimed to have been the only person in history to create a written language without at the same time being fluent in another one.

Events leading up to the 1838 "Trail of Tears" are described. The proclamation to the Cherokees by US General Winfield Scott, charged with the responsibility for the actual roundup and transfer of the tribe to Oklahoma, brings that sad time home with a vengeance. In a darkened room off the main museum display area a variety of photographs of Cherokees, some dating well back into the last century, I found particularly moving.

The last exhibit is a well-made film of the Cherokee Tribe today. Despite the tragic periods in Cherokee history— Rutherford's invasion is one—the tribe's future, based on what I saw in the movie, seems bright. I found it interesting that the number of tribal members in North Carolina today, about nine thousand, is approximately half the number thought to have been living on the land when the white man first showed up.

I recommend a visit to the museum. For me it was well worth the rather steep entrance fee. As in just about every

105

other pool of history I splash through on Carolina rambles, my introduction to the Cherokees will send me to the library to learn more.

# A Doorstop That Changed History—The Reed Gold Mine

CONRAD REED LIKED TO PLAY in Little Meadow Creek, a meandering shallow stream on his family's farm in the rolling country east of Charlotte. One day in 1799 the nine-year-old boy found a pretty yellow rock in the creek. His mother agreed that the rock, which weighed seventeen pounds, was pretty. She used it as a doorstop for several years. It was pure gold.

Conrad Reed's creek-find turned out to be the first gold discovered in the United States. It precipitated the first gold rush in the country and started the industry that was for a time to employ more people in North Carolina than any other except farming.

John Reed, Conrad's father, in 1802 sold the yellow rock for the princely sum of $3.50 to a jeweler in Fayetteville. The jeweler then sold it for $3500. Today it would be worth about $100,000.

John Reed got smarter. He began exploring Little Meadow Creek for more gold. He found it, formed a company to mine it and died a rich man in 1845. Commercial gold mining continued at the Reed farm, with interruptions for the Civil War and inheritance squabbles, until 1912. During the Depression in this century the spoils from earlier mining were reworked by hungry men looking for stray nuggets.

According to the guide for my tour of the site, the white quartz ore remaining there today contains gold worth about 60 cents per ton of quartz. He also told of the finding, in early days, of a 28 pound nugget in the creek. Imagine that.

I visited the Reed Gold Mine, a state historical site, on a very hot day in June. I drove down from Asheville on US 74, through Hickory Nut Gorge and Lake Lure, to hazy, blistering Charlotte. There, a left turn onto NC 49 brought me to Cabarrus County and, after some twenty miles, to NC 601. A few miles north on 601 through neat, sparsely populated farm land brought me to the Reed Mine.

A recently built museum stands on the site, on the banks of Little Meadow Creek. A slide show in the museum tells the story of gold in North Carolina. Exhibits show the evolution of gold mining technology. In the museum several open safes in plastic cases contain gold objects, from nuggets to coins to jewelry to bottles of gold-containing chemicals. I presume the safes are locked at night.

From the museum frequent guided tours cross a bridge over Little Meadow Creek and enter the underground workings of the mine. I paused on the bridge and looked hard at every rock that I could see in the creek but, alas, saw no yellow glints. (I wonder how many people in the last two centuries have looked for yellow in those very same rocks.)

We entered a horizontal tunnel in the side of a hill. The tunnel mouth is lined with white quartz, gold ore. A sign requests that you not remove the quartz. The air temperature outside the tunnel on the day of my visit was 95 degrees. The wind pouring from the tunnel was 55 degrees.

Inside the earth the played-out quartz veins in the damp, dripping walls are clearly visible. We saw the vertical shafts where workers, many of them miners brought over from Cornwall in England, entered the mine in leather buckets let down from above. Delicate little subterranean green plants grow under the tunnel lights. Everything underground is cold and wet. I was glad to return to the sun.

You may sit under a shed near the tunnel exit and pan for nuggets. Three dollars buys you a bucket of ore, instructions and the use of a placer pan.

The Reed Mine is maintained in part by the Gold History Corporation, a local organization which you may join. Application forms are available at the museum.

I enjoyed my visit to the Reed Mine. The site is well maintained and a lot of history is to be learned there. The staff is knowledgeable and helpful. No fee is charged. My only disappointment was that I found no nuggets. I wasn't expecting a seventeen pounder, you understand, but a simple little *one*-pounder wouldn't be too unreasonable, do you think?

# The Outer Banks—From Duck To The End Of The Road

Want to get away from it all, but not go *too* far? Well, get in your four-wheel-drive and unfold your map. We're going to a place where the only road ends in a pile of sand but traffic doesn't stop, where miles from *any* road the speed limit is still 35 miles per hour, to a place where whole communities exist with no roads at all leading to them, where ospreys and pelicans patrol the surf and wild horses eat your garbage. I spent a week there and I'm ready to go back. To get there is easy.

From anywhere in North Carolina just seek out US 64 on its 500 plus mile trek through the length of the state and turn toward the rising sun. Drive east until you cross the Alligator River, pass through Manteo, smell salt marsh and hear the ocean's roar. There, where at Whalebone Junction US 64 finally ends, you are on North Carolina's fabled Outer Banks, where Blackbeard scoured the sea and the Wright brothers pulled the world into the age of flight. The spindly barrier islands are traditionally referred to in tourist literature as the "*lonely*, windswept Outer Banks".

Well, the wind still sweeps. But today, at least in tourist season, you have to get up pretty early in the morning if you want to be alone on the beach. The banks have been *discovered*. Never mind, we're going beyond all that.

At Whalebone Junction turn left, north, hug the beach, and keep going. Perhaps you will want to stop for lunch at one of the many quaint, short-lived restaurants that pepper the highway, places with names like "Ye Olde Pirate's Cove Deli" or "Wilde Duck Dunes Pizzeria and Seashell Shop". After lunch watch out for traffic and keep going north, to Duck.

Until recent times Duck was the jumping-off place, the end, the point where lonely really started. No longer. Today you must grip your steering wheel and thread a way through the bikers, striders, joggers, dawdlers and cruisers that clog the road. Discouraged? Don't be. Keep going.

The first indication that the end of the road is near is a roadside sign, fifteen miles north of Duck, that warns drivers to watch out for wild horses. Look sharp and you may see a few of them grazing near the road as you pass. Stay on the pavement, though. The sand here can swallow a car and not even burp. Two miles further the old red brick tower of Corolla lighthouse rises above scrubby pines on your left. A couple of miles more and you are stopped abruptly by a large sand dune that covers the roadway. Beyond the dune beach vegetation stretches, unbroken, as far as you can see.

No, you didn't miss a turn. This is the end of the road. Or is it?

On the day of my first visit to the road's end I heard, over the rumble and crash of the surf, a roar. Then a rusty pickup truck churned through the sand in a gap in the dunes on my right, thumped onto the pavement behind me and headed Duckward. Another followed a minute later. Both trucks carried the symbol of the true Outer Banker, a rack of six or eight monster fishing rods mounted vertically like flags across the truck fronts.

Another pickup came up the paved road behind me and disappeared through the dunes onto the beach. Then a large truck—a *moving van*!—ground up through the gap from the beach, bumped onto the pavement and headed south. I walked over the dune to the beach to see where it had come from. Up out of the ocean, maybe?

I learned that the highway certainly does end there where the pavement stops, but who needs pavement? From there up to Virginia, some fifteen miles north, the beach is the road, the *only* road. A large sign mounted in the sand near the high tide mark displays the traffic rules for Currituck County. It tells that all vehicles are prohibited from the beach south of the sign from May 1 through September 30. A sheriff's van enforces the beach-traffic rules. The speed limit posted at frequent intervals up the beach from where I stood is 35 miles per hour.

Day and night a variety of vehicles use the beach-road. Many carry people on holiday—fishermen, picnickers or tourists with new four-wheel-drive vans eager to be tested in deep sand. Many other vehicles, however, carry *commuters*.

Five miles north of the road-end two small communities, Carova and Swan, sit on the sand and face the ocean. Electricity they have, but no roads! The only access to Carova and Swan is by beach. The stream of traffic you meet on early morning beach walks is people going to work. Going, I suppose, to build and staff the pizzerias and delis further south.

Why has a road not been built to Carova and Swan and on up to Virginia? you ask. Why must these people drive on the sand?

I was told that the Audubon Society owns a strip of the banks north of Corolla and will not let a highway be built across their land. Hooray for them! I fervently hope that progress never moves beyond Corolla lighthouse, that Currituck's wild horses never become developed. Ah, yes, those horses.

A small herd, descendants of mustangs left four centuries ago by Spanish explorers, roams freely from Corolla north into Virginia. Unfettered and unfenced they wander, tourist attractions of the first magnitude. Unfortunately they often wander onto the highway at Corolla. Six of the horses were killed by cars last summer. One hot July afternoon I saw the kind of horse-traffic interaction that occurs.

Just south of Corolla eight horses grazed in a patch of beach grass near the road. Eleven cars had stopped on the pavement or pulled off into the sand. A semicircle of cameras clicked and whirred at the unconcerned animals. Mothers gripped children. One Pennsylvania station wagon was stuck up to its bumper in the sand, others would surely become stuck when they tried to move. I wonder what horse thoughts the members of the herd have when awkward two-legged creatures follow them around most of the day waving little boxes at them.

Currituck horses are protected by law. Like the sacred cows of India, they roam where they will. One morning before sunup as I watched the day's first ospreys and pelicans from the deck of our vacation house, a wild horse family—stallion, mare and young colt—came out of the scrub. The walnut-colored patriarch of the little clan went to our garbage can, which was overflowing on this pick-up day, and nudged until the can tipped over. The mare and colt then came to the spilled contents and all three horses searched for morsels of lettuce or corn shucks. Next year I'll leave any fodder outside the can to save them trouble.

Despite beach commuters the land north of Duck is not crowded. It's certainly still windswept and maybe even a little lonely at times, but change is at work. Several sprawling resorts are being built near the Corolla lighthouse. Tasteful, with constantly watered lawns and flower beds, they ooze from sound to sea. Soon Corolla will resemble Duck. I was told that a bridge is to be built from the mainland, bringing Corolla a hundred miles closer to New Jersey, Pennsylvania, New York. Well, so be it. Progress must continue its thrilling march, but still...

May the Audubon Society remain steadfast. May a road never make the Carovian's and Swanian's commute easier. May my wild horse family never be penned.

# Shrimpboats And Steel Mills—Georgetown.

Between glitzy Myrtle Beach to the north and staid Charleston to the south, on a peninsula bounded by Winyah Bay and Sampit Creek, lies the port city of Georgetown. My wife and I recently attended a wedding there and I had the opportunity to ramble. I found Georgetown and the area around it to be a surprising mixture of old and new, of history, tourism and heavy industry.

Shrimp boats still dock off Front Street in Historic Seaport Georgetown on the east bank of Sampit Creek, as they have for two and a half centuries. Behind Front Street lies the old town as it was laid out by the British in the early 1700s, a rectangular grid of streets with names like King, Queen, Prince and Duke, where many houses date from the town's early years. Huge live oak trees provided dappled shade on the sunny day of my walk-around. Several two-centuries-old churches with brick-walled cemeteries are within a few blocks of the waterfront.

The restored Front Street business district has shops and restaurants, little parks and walkways and shady places to sit. Here the Rice Museum tells of Georgetown's glory years, the period in the early 1800s when two crops, rice and indigo, made Georgetown County "the richest in the nation." A boardwalk along the harbor runs the length of the restored area. If you stand on the boardwalk, face east and ignore automobiles and a few other modern intrusions, you will look backward in time two hundred years. Turn around and you face today.

A short distance up Sampit Creek a dark mountain rises, with smoke and steam and noise coming from it. The mountain is Georgetown Steel mill, producer of specialty steel products—Georgetown's rice and indigo of our time, I suppose. A sprawling paper mill lies beyond the steel mill. I don't know how manufacturing and tourism rank in the overall economy of the region, but to have both industries healthy is surely a good sign for the town.

The wedding we attended was held in Prince George Episcopal Church in the historic district. The church building, which stands at the corner of its shaded cemetery, dates from about 1750. Inside the church worn stone floors in the aisles divide ranks of walled pews, each with its own gate.

Benches are attached to the walls inside the pews. Some of the benches face forward, some to the side, some to the rear. The walls are high enough so that small children cannot see over them. Listening to long sermons while sitting on a hard bench in a wooden box, perhaps facing backwards, perhaps cold, must have been of signal value to the character of the citizens of old Georgetown. Only a few initials were carved in the wood of the pew that I sat in, none of them very old.

I was told that the pew walls were there to aid in keeping the pews warm in winter. Little charcoal burners were used as heaters. The church itself was never heated. The altar and furnishings in the high-ceilinged sanctuary are simple but impressive.

A brochure states that the British stabled their horses in the church building during their occupation of the town in 1780, after the fall of Charleston to Cornwallis's army. The graves of two British soldiers are said to be in the cemetery. I found tombstones with dates from that period but did not identify those of the British soldiers. Francis Marion, South Carolina's Swamp Fox, after several bloody attempts, drove the Redcoats out of Georgetown in 1781.

Georgetown was an important supply port for the Confederacy during the Civil War and was subject to a blockade by the Union navy for much of the period. Late in the war the city was occupied by Union troops. In March 1865, very near the end of the fighting, the flagship of the Union fleet operating out of Georgetown, the USS Harvest Moon, was sunk in Winyah bay by a Confederate torpedo.

After the war the plantation economy of the region, which was based on slave labor, collapsed. Soon the rice and indigo fields returned to the wild, to be replaced, in time, by tourists and steel mills. And here and there, I was told, by kiwi fruit plantations.

Leaving Georgetown on US 17 north, you cross the head of Winyah Bay onto a long peninsula known as Waccamaw Neck. Here expensive golf resorts with names like "Debedieu"—pronounced, as best I could hear it, "Debby-doo"—hide behind gilded, landscaped entrance gates and guard houses that are manned twenty-four hours a day. Less pretentious communities like Pawley's Island provide public beach access.

Famous Brookgreen Gardens is on US 17 about ten miles north of Georgetown. Brookgreen is laid out in an old rice plantation, and displays what is claimed to be the largest collection of American sculpture in the world. If you stop there, plan to spend at least two or three hours.

A few miles further is Murrell's Inlet, a several-mile-long succession of seafood restaurants. On the Friday night of our visit almost every parking lot was jammed and traffic was a problem. A motorcyclist convention a few miles north in Myrtle Beach coincided with our evening in Murrell's Inlet. Harley-Davidsons were as thick as sandpeas on the beach. The seafood was only fair and was high-priced.

I was glad to return to the mountains.

# Don't Step On The PhDs—
# Durham, Duke Homestead
# And The Research Triangle

A COUPLE OF HOURS IN NORTH Carolina's City of Medicine will make real for you an incredible century of history. You can move from Washington Duke's first tobacco factory, a garage-sized shed in the pines where Wash and his sons ground tobacco by hand, to the very froth on the wave of the future, Research Triangle Park. From a time and place where brooms were made of corn stalks and toothbrushes of sweetgum twigs, to super computers and miracle drugs. Where, it's reported, there are more Ph.D.s per square yard than anywhere else in the world.

So watch where you put your feet.

It's all happened in a little over a hundred years, less than two lifetimes. Nowhere that I have been is the crunch of technology more apparent than it is in Durham.

Four hours due east from Asheville on I-40, through Winston-Salem and Greensboro, then north on I-85, you reach the City of Medicine, so called because of all the medical research centered at Duke University. Most Durhamites prefer that nickname to another, more common, "Bull City." I suggest that you start your visit at Duke Homestead Park, a mile or so north of I-85 on Duke Homestead Road.

You can pick up a copy of the Durham Visitor's Guide there. You'll need one. The guide at the time of my visit listed nine pages of places and things to do and see in the city and surrounding country, from sixteen art galleries to thirty-four historic places and landmarks, with whole pages of science and nature in between. But for now put the visitor's guide away and concentrate on the world of Washington Duke.

Plan to take your time at the Homestead. There's a lot more there than just the story of Carolina bright leaf and cigarettes. A guide will lead you through the restored Duke tobacco farm and through the house as it was a hundred years ago. You will hear how tobacco was grown and processed then and now, see trundle beds in small bedrooms where people slept in the days when everybody worked from "can't see to can't see," and walk through a typical kitchen of North Carolina in the late nineteenth century, shortly after the fireplace had been replaced with a modern castiron woodstove.

The farm tour ends at the museum. Before visiting the exhibits there, watch the introductory twenty-minute film, well done, that shows life on a tobacco farm in the time of Model Ts and then jumps forward to today. A mild bias toward tobacco-growing as a good life pervades the film, but not excessively. After the movie, walk through the extensive exhibit area, where audio and visual effects display all aspects of tobacco history and technology. More interesting than the advance of machines and mass production to me was the section of the museum dealing with advertising and promotion of American Tobacco Company's products.

Radio commercials from early days play at the touch of a button, and later TV commercials show on screens. "L S M F T, Lucky Strike Means Fine Tobacco." Remember that? It's almost shocking today to hear the smarmy, wheedling, purring announcers of an earlier time urging the audience to smoke.

More has changed in the industry than just cigarette manufacturing procedures.

Another aspect of tobacco history is the way American Tobacco Company got started. Washington Duke "made acquisitions," to use today's words. He simply made an offer to each of his competitors that few could bring themselves to refuse for long: "Join me or I'll drive you out of business." Soon Duke controlled almost all of the burgeoning tobacco industry. Money began to cascade into Durham from all over the world.

Early in this century the federal government broke up American Tobacco's monopoly, but not before Duke University, Duke Power and many of the textile giants of the region were founded, before charities of all kinds benefited. I wonder. What if old Wash Duke had been less aggressive in business, had been satisfied with a *little* tobacco company? Would the national basketball champs live in Durham today? Would Duke University still be little Trinity College? Would...

But, no, don't speculate. It's a waste of time. Let's move on forward to today.

The Research Triangle Park, which fills much of the area bounded by Durham, Raleigh and Chapel Hill, is by almost any yardstick the most successful such venture in the world. I was a student at Chapel Hill when then-governor Luther Hodges, later to become John Kennedy's Secretary of Commerce, proposed the park. I remember being very skeptical of the whole venture at the time. Luckily for the state—and the nation—those responsible for the park were not so wishy-washy as I.

From early beginnings, when the US Forest Service, the park's first tenant, built a research lab, the park has grown steadily. Today over fifty tenants, including IBM, GE, Dupont, and Borroughs-Wellcome, employ 33,000 people, making the

"Triangle Area" one of the premier places for technology in the world.

Burroughs-Wellcome's distinctive laboratory buildings catch the eye as you drive through the park. My first thought when I saw them was of a fort on the Maginot line, but I had missed the point completely. The buildings were designed, not to defend, but to blend with their bucolic surroundings, like an old North Carolina farm house that had just kept growing. The architect described his creation as "a stack of front porches."

Drive through the park, just wander around. Avoid rush hours in the morning and afternoon, though. See the future in the modern, functional, working structures—today's factories—partly hidden in the Carolina woods of the park.

Then think back a hundred years, to Washington Duke's first tobacco factory, to his screens and hand grinding. Now try to imagine what changes two *more* lifetimes will bring to North Carolina and the world.

# Culture By The Fairgrounds— The North Carolina Museum Of Art

A LOW CONCRETE BUILDING reminiscent of a World War II pillbox stands in the area between I-40 and the North Carolina state fairgrounds, a few miles west of Raleigh. A large bronze statue of smooth flowing curves and sharp points near the building's entrance could from a distance easily be mistaken for cannons or machine guns, perhaps there to protect the pillbox from a nearby youth prison complex. This warlike impression is wrong, though.

The uncompromising gray structure houses the North Carolina Museum of Art, a treasure not well known, as far as I can tell, in the outer reaches of the state where I live. It should be.

My wife and I visited the museum on a sunny Monday in May. We got there shortly after the doors opened.

Now, I think I should at this point admit to you that I am, for the most part, an unredeemable cynic on the subject of ART. I'm ready with nicely curled lip at the first sign of anything called "abstract," and am not in the least overwhelmed by pictures of bulgy naked women or ancient saints. Or of witch doctor masks. I planned a ten-minute walk-through of the museum. Just so I could say that I had been there.

Well, we stayed all morning, didn't see half of what's on display, and intend to return whenever we're in the area.

Oh, I got my chances to sneer at abstracts, and bulgy ladies and witch doctor masks are there in plenty. But there is much, much more. We will go back and, next time, wander through the honeycomb of galleries slowly. Who knows? I might even, in the fullness of time, uncurl my abstract lip a bit.

The museum, or at least the idea for the museum, dates back to 1947, when North Carolina became the first state in the nation to establish an art collection with public funds, a million dollars to match a grant by philanthropist Samuel Kress. The early collection was housed in a converted Raleigh office building. The present museum, completed in 1983, was designed by the architect who was responsible for the Kennedy Center in Washington.

The museum, which is built on a downward slope, is much larger than it appears from the front. The entrance is on the top floor, with two others below. Permanent collections of American, Classical, Egyptian, European and Twentieth Century Art are on the top two floors, as were, at the time of my visit, collections from Jewish, African, Oceanic and New World cultures.

The lower level is used for changing exhibits. We saw "The Naked Soul: Polish Paintings from the National Museum, Poznan." On the top floor an exhibit called "From the Ground Up, Experiencing Architecture" describes in detail the creation of the museum building, from site selection through construction.

The museum was busy but uncrowded the day we visited. Many attendants, mostly volunteers, staff the information desk, gift shop and cafe. Guided tours are available. There is no admission charge. By the time we left just before noon, school buses had started unloading large, well-accompanied coveys of fifth graders. The uniformed attendants (guards?) in each of the galleries looked bored even early in the morning. I never saw one sitting down.

Okay, so how far did my lip curl in the Twentieth Century section? Not too far. I still can't answer the question: "But is it *ART*?" but I did decide that there is one characteristic of the items on display that I can assess. How long did it take the artist to create—not to plan for, but actually to make—the painting, sculpture, etc.?

You might well ask what difference it makes how long it took. Maybe none, but... Most of the older paintings look like years of work; some of the modern ones *couldn't* have taken even many minutes. Decades of planning, soul-searching and study by the artist may have gone into getting ready, but the actual putting of paint on canvas could have, I believe, been done between coffee breaks.

Remember "The Emperor's New Clothes"?

But, enough of that. Too much, probably. I am definitely not an art critic.

Suffice it to say that, naked emperor or not, I am eager to go back to the museum and look some more.

# Kings Mountain—
# British Bayonets In The
# Carolina Woods

On a misty October afternoon in 1780, on a South Carolina hill grandly named Kings Mountain, more than 2000 men fought a battle that changed the course of history. One half of the men that day fought, at least nominally, for the cause of independence, the other half for the King. But all of the men on the mountain, with the exception of one lone Scotsman, were Americans.

Here in the Carolina back country the Revolutionary War was mostly neighbor-against-neighbor, friend-against-friend, a civil war. The fighting was particularly cruel and gruesome. The passing of two centuries has dimmed the horror of that time in our history, but a visit to Kings Mountain will give a glimpse of the way it was.

Kings Mountain Military Park is five miles south of Interstate 85, just below the NC-SC line. A visitor center with a museum and a twenty-minute film about the battle stands near the actual site of the fighting, a 60-foot-high, flat-topped, tree-covered hill, Kings Mountain. From the visitor center a mile-long paved trail winds around the hill, first through ground occupied by the Americans then through the British positions, before returning to the visitor center.

A stroll through the quiet woods of Kings Mountain is pleasant and informative, but it fails in its main purpose. Neither the trail nor the museum nor the movie nor even Ferguson's grave can make real for us today that desperate scene from two centuries ago. We can't bring back the hell of gunfire and smoke, the shouts of fighters and screams from wounded and dying. But though we may not be able to relive the battle, I think we should at least try. We owe it to the Americans who fought there. If it hadn't been for them, we just might today, as they still do in Canada, toast the Queen rather than salute the flag.

After five draining years of war, the American independence cause badly needed a victory. The war in the north had by the end of the 1770s settled into stalemate, with the British holding New York and the other major ports, and the Americans the countryside. Neither army could dislodge the other, but as privations in the country mounted, the will of the Americans began to soften.

The British decided to break the stalemate and end the war by directing their campaign to the south. They would overrun the southern colonies, which had until then been little involved in the war, then move northward from a secure base to squeeze George Washington and put finish to the revolution. To this end they assembled an army, appointed Earl Charles Cornwallis its commander, gathered a fleet to transport the army, and sailed south. For more than a year their southern strategy proceeded just as the generals had drawn it up. Final defeat of the Americans seemed only a matter of time, and not much time at that.

In the initial push south, the British had easily taken Savannah following a landing from the sea. Then in 1780 Charleston and most of South Carolina fell. With Cornwallis threatening to sweep the Carolinas and move into Virginia,

Washington dispatched a rescuing army under General Horatio Gates to South Carolina. Gates met Cornwallis at Camden, where the American army was annihilated in the worst defeat suffered by the Patriots during the entire war. The way north lay open to the Redcoats.

As Cornwallis, headquartered in the village of Charlotte, prepared for the planned war-ending northern push, elements of his army patrolled the Carolina countryside. What organized resistance remained retreated to the foothills and mountains to the west. Tories, who had been mostly silent for the past five years, emerged in the towns as Patriots evaporated. To many waverers among the citizenry, it appeared certain that the British would win the war. King George daily regained loyal subjects who had foolishly strayed from the flock but now wanted back in. Only the rabble in the west remained as potential trouble.

In one of the mistakes that shape history, Cornwallis ordered a fiery Scotsman, Major Patrick Ferguson—"Bulldog" to his troops—to end the western threat. Ferguson, commander of all loyalist forces in the Carolinas, sent word that unless the "over-mountain" men ceased resistance, he would cross the mountains, hang their leaders and lay waste to their lands "with fire and sword."

Response to the threat was immediate. Instead of laying down arms, angry men took tighter hold of their long rifles and began to move down from the mountain coves and valleys of the Carolinas, Tennessee and Virginia. They gathered around leaders like Isaac Shelby, John Sevier, Charles McDowell and William Campbell and set out from a place called Sycamore Flats on the Watauga River, across the ridges in search of Major Ferguson. They found him at Kings Mountain.

The details of the battle that followed, of Ferguson's

death and the total defeat of the 1000 men under him, is well told at the visitor center and on the trail. The Americans surrounded the hill where Ferguson had dug in, then began to climb in the face of concerted musket fire. In the British tradition of fighting, Ferguson ordered a bayonet charge. The Americans backed off—turned and ran is more accurate—but when the British stopped and turned back toward their lines, the mountain men's long squirrel rifles spoke. Deadly at 300 yards, the guns in hands of men who hunted to live had little trouble killing red-coated men scrambling up a hill at close range. Within an hour the battle was over.

When he realized that defeat was inevitable, Ferguson made a dash for freedom on his horse, but was cut down by three bullets. He was buried where he fell, in a rocky cairn as was the custom in his native Scotland. The cairn lies today close by the trail.

Twenty-eight Americans were killed at Kings Mountain. British losses included more than 200 killed during the battle—and after. White flags were ignored long after British resistance ended. Many men trying to surrender were shot. Later, as the British were being taken to the Continental headquarters at Hillsborough, more were hanged.

The overwhelming victory at Kings Mountain breathed life back into our fight for independence. A few months after Kings Mountain the British were again badly beaten at Cowpens, not 30 miles from the earlier battle. Resistance stiffened everywhere in the Carolinas.

Cornwallis moved north as planned and in fact ended the war, as planned. But he ended it by surrendering to—not defeating—George Washington. Kings Mountain had been the turning point, the first step toward Yorktown.

# Where Daniel Morgan Turned The Tide Of War— Cowpens Battleground

On a cold, bright January morning in 1781, at a clearing in the woods known by the unlovely name of Hannah's Cowpens, a group of men hurried to bury the bodies of 114 British soldiers in pits that had been dug by farmers to trap wolves. The task completed they gathered supply wagons and two small brass cannons captured from the British. Then, herding 500 prisoners before them, they ran for their lives. Cornwallis was coming, and no quarter would be given if he caught them.

In upstate South Carolina, at a place where farmers assembled cattle before sending them to market, a place of thinly spaced trees well suited for cavalry operations, brawler Daniel Morgan had just breathed life into the dying cause of revolution. With a ragged force of about a thousand men, he had destroyed a feared and hated British unit of seasoned regular infantry, cavalry and artillery known as Tarleton's Legion.

Morgan's unexpected victory was to send a charge of hope to the war-weary northern colonies. The triumph, following close on the victory at Kings Mountain three months earlier, would cause the strengthening of General Nathaniel Greene's collapsing Southern Army and would, within eight months, lead to the surrender of the British at Yorktown. None of this was apparent to Morgan's ill-matched militiamen from six colonies on that frosty morning as they scrambled to escape the avenging army sure to be sent by Cornwallis, who was camped with the main British force just 25 miles away in the direction of Charlotte.

Cowpens Battlefield Site, operated by the National Park Service, is near I-85, just east of the town of Chesnee, not far from Gaffney's famous peach-shaped water tank. For me it was an easy hour-and-a-half drive from Asheville: I-26 down the mountain, then east on SC 11 through 20 miles of peach orchards, pasture land and woods to Cowpens Battlefield Park.

You should start a visit at the modern visitor center, where weapons and uniforms of the day are displayed and an illuminated map and slide show tell of troop movements and events of the battle. Then take a well-maintained mile-long paved trail from the visitor center to the places where the fighting occurred. Maps and recorded messages at intervals describe the action of that long-ago day.

Look for wildlife as you stroll. On my late September visit I saw tracks of fox and deer, and many songbirds. A pileated woodpecker flew across the trail just in front of me. I sampled a few black sour-sweet muscadine grapes that still clung to vines in the trailside brush.

The uncrowded park is open all year and is kept well-groomed. There is no entrance fee, though a dollar is charged for the slide show, which is well worth the price. A shady picnic area is near the visitor center. A visit to Cowpens is a pleasant way to spend the day.

But if you go there, try to look beyond the flower beds, neat lawns and picnickers. Look back a couple of centuries. Imagine the sights, sounds and smells of that cold dawn in

1781. Stand on the slope where Morgan's line waited. Try to see through the eyes of a boy in the line. Imagine that you are sixteen years old. Feel the weight of the musket in your cold sweating hands. Listen to your heart pounding. Breath the icy air. Imagine.

*Be* that boy!

See the redcoats emerge from the woods across the broad meadow, see the glint of their bayonets in the low winter sun. Hear the stomp and clatter of British cavalry waiting the order to charge. Know that they are going to come crashing toward you! Hear the wail of bagpipes.

The redcoats form their line and begin to move toward you in the Britisher's standard shuffling half-trot that had struck terror into so many of King's enemies in the past. A cannon booms, then another. You hear the shot crash through the bare limbs above your head.

What are you going to do now, boy?

Above all things, don't run! Wait. Don't shoot until they are a hundred paces away. Then aim—remember to aim!—and shoot. Aim to kill. Aim low. Aim for the ones wearing epaulets. Kill the officers. Then reload and shoot again. *Then* run!

"Just two shots, boys!" General Morgan had told you and your fellows, over and over, the night before. "Two good shots, then run behind the next line. Two shots. That's all I want."

Well, you didn't run. Morgan's plan worked. His militia line held, fired twice, then scurried away. The British, seeing the rebels' flight as expected panic, came on. Morgan's second line, then his third, fired. Squirrel hunters from the frontier found the red-coated men at close range easy targets. In the smoke and shriek of battle, mistakes were made on both sides and confusion swept away preset plans. But on that day it was the disciplined British who, only minutes after the fight started, threw down their muskets and ran, not Morgan's backwoods rabble.

Tarleton barely escaped with a handful of men, but his legion, which had terrorized South Carolina, was destroyed. Cornwallis's plan to separate the southern colonies from those in the north received a blow from which it would not recover. The roots of Yorktown took hold.

The importance given to Cowpens at the time is shown by the fact that, of only twelve medals struck after the war by Congress to honor those who fought in the Revolution, three were awarded to participants at Cowpens.

We don't often think about the Revolutionary War these days. Scenes of Washington crossing the Delaware or freezing at Valley Forge are part of our heritage, but the brutal war in the South is largely unknown. In the Carolinas it was a civil war, a war of ambush and terror fought mostly by small bands of men, a war waged on impossible terrain of endless ridges, creeks and swamps, where roads were scarce and food often scarcer, a war with no right and wrong. Both loyalists and rebels fought as patriots to their cause. Cowpens was part of that war.

After the battle, Daniel Morgan retired to his Virginia home, finally crippled by the sciatica that had plagued him for years.

Banastre Tarleton returned to the fight and remained Cornwallis's trusted second. Several months after Cowpens he led a dash into Virginia in an unsuccessful attempt to capture Thomas Jefferson at Charlottesville. (An ancient tree from that time, called Tarleton's Oak, still stands in a little park in downtown Charlottesville.) Tarleton surrendered with Cornwallis at Yorktown. After the war he returned to England, became a member of Parliament, was knighted, and lived to be an old man.

Questions of "What if?" are inexcusable wastes of time, but...

What if you, that boy in Morgan's first line, had thrown down your gun and run? Might that not have led to the panic that the British looked for? And with panic, mightn't the King's cavalry have swept the field? Wouldn't the dead and prisoners of that day have been American, not British? Would we today toast the Queen rather than salute the flag?

If we had failed at Cowpens, would the French Revolution that followed our own have happened in the way that it did? Would we even recognize the world today? What if...

Go to Cowpens, relive that desperate hour, and ponder. Perhaps give a little extra thanks to the boy with the musket. The boy who didn't run.

# Ninety Six—Trading Post, Frontier Fort And Unconquered British Stronghold

DURING THE TEN THOUSAND years or so that Indians lived in Carolina without the help of Europeans, they moved around. Trading, hunting, fighting, visiting relatives, maybe just rambling, Cherokees and their neighbors walked (horses not being part of their culture) through mountain passes, beside rivers, up and down valleys. Well-worn paths evolved along the best routes. After Charleston and other European settlements formed along the coast in the late 1600s, trade between Indians and whites grew rapidly and travel on the forest paths increased accordingly.

Indians early developed a want for knives, beads, cloth, guns, firewater—all things they had gotten along well without since their time on earth began. The settlers wanted in return products of the forest, animal hides in particular. White traders started moving up the Indian paths to get closer to their source of supply. A man named Robert Gouedy built a trading post in 1751 on the path that led from Cherokee lands in the foothills down to Charleston, at a place where the Charleston path intersected several others. Gouedy's store was well-sited. It prospered and acquired a name, Ninety Six.

Why Ninety Six? Why not Gouedytown? The name was drawn from the fact that Gouedy's trading post was ninety-six miles from Keowee, a major Cherokee town near today's Greenville. (I wonder how they measured trail distances in those days.)

White settlers began to occupy the land around Ninety Six. A village grew at Gouedy's store. Cabins were built on nearby fertile creek bottom land, woods were cleared for plowing, game was killed, and the old, painful, inevitable frontier story was told again.

Friction developed between settlers and Cherokees. Fights occurred. Gouedy fortified his store with a stockade and it became a refuge for settlers during increasingly frequent Cherokee raids. Up and down the Carolina frontier people were killed, both settlers and Indians. Each killing called for revenge.

This outbreak of frontier fighting occurred at a time when a larger conflict was rising in the region as France disputed Britain's hold on eastern North America. The French sought help from the Cherokees. Tribal leaders listened and decided to take up arms and drive the British from their land. (A decade later, in another bad decision, the Cherokees would side *with* the British in an effort to drive the Americans out.) What followed, on a grand scale, is known as the French and Indian War. In the Carolina backcountry, where questions of world politics mattered little, it was the Cherokee War.

Early in 1760, just nine years after Gouedy built his store, the Cherokees launched simultaneous raids on settlers along the whole length of the frontier. Gouedy's fort became a prime target and, for the next twenty violent years, remained one. During the Revolutionary War that followed on the heels of the French and Indian one, the British built a fort at Ninety Six. George Washington's Southern commander, General

Greene, laid siege to the fort in what became known as the Battle of Ninety Six.

Today a national park preserves the site of that battle. I decided to go there and turn another page in my personal Carolina history book.

On a still, clear Sunday morning in early December I left Asheville and followed I-26 south for about seventy-five miles down into South Carolina's "Upcountry." At SC 72 I left the Interstate, turned right, passed through the town of Clinton, home of Presbyterian College, and continued westward toward the Saluda River.

Hazy sunshine had melted morning frost by that time, turning the early chill into a perfect soft Carolina winter day, the kind of weather chambers of commerce dream of. Mist rose from glass-smooth farm ponds along the way, ponds set in beige, brown and rust winter pastures. A few people dressed for church were on the road, but for the most part the country was mine. In the yards around many homes along the highway were those quintessential Carolina symbols, pecan trees and gray tangles of leafless scuppernong vines. Huge old oak trees, winter-green with clumps of mistletoe, spread over front yards. The air warmed enough for me to leave a car window open. The clean December air smelled of pine. People in shirt sleeves were decorating house fronts for Christmas.

Two miles beyond the Saluda River, which is actually the upper reaches of Lake Greenwood at this point, I turned left on SC 246 toward Ninety Six. I passed a huge new-looking Fuji Film factory, its parking lot full even on Sunday morning. Signs along the roadside told that Fuji Film keeps that section litter-free. The up-and-down piedmont country had flattened beyond the Saluda, and fields on both sides were green with winter wheat.

Three miles more and I reached Ninety Six, a town of some two thousand citizens. Sunday morning calm covered the town center, where a new gazebo sat in a grassy plot next to a spruced-up railroad station. Across from the station a straight row of about a dozen stores, their vertical fronts evoking the 1930s, lined Main Street. The gazebo and train station were bright with red and green Christmas decorations. A sign at the Town Hall told of paintings of the Battle of Ninety Six on display inside, admission free. The building was closed on Sunday.

From the town, following signs, I drove three miles west on SC 248 to the object of the day's ramble, The Ninety Six National Historic Site, and stopped in the paved parking area by the park headquarters. A friendly-looking little cannon from the battle commanded the path to the nearby brown wooden visitor center.

Inside the visitor center I found a museum room on the left, a slide theater on the right. A knowledgeable ranger showed me a rather fuzzy eight minute video history of Ninety Six. After the show I left the building and entered the trail that winds through the actual battle site. After an easy half mile through winter-bare woods the trail emerged from a shallow valley onto a section of the old Cherokee trading path, which lies in a depression in the ground several feet deep and about twenty feet wide. I wondered why it is in a trough. The ground there is level, so water erosion would not seem to have been a major factor. Could it be that ten thousand years of Indian moccasins simply wore the earth away? Probably not.

From the old trading path the park trail opens onto a broad, treeless grassy area, winter beige on the day of my visit, then leads in a series of curves through Greene's siege works to the reconstructed star-shaped array of earthen walls of the

British fort. The fort's shape was such that fire from the star's points commanded all of the exterior fort walls.

Cannons aimed at the fort were placed along the path. Deer tracks were everywhere. A breeze rattled dead brown leaves left in the top of a nearby oak, the sound loud in the silence of the winter day. The story of the battle is told on signs along the path. I was impressed by how *small* the whole area of fighting was. A replica of Greene's assault tower, built during darkness with logs cut during the day, stands near the fort. The tower allowed Greene's riflemen to fire down on the British inside the walls.

From the star fort the trail passes through the town site, level now with no visible remains of the courthouse, jail or other buildings of the time. Half mile further is a reconstructed stockade, part of the British defenses and site of an earlier skirmish that saw the first deaths—the first of a great many—of the Revolution in South Carolina. From the stockade the trail leads back to the visitor center. My cool December day having become downright hot, I sat in the shade of a large cedar to think over what I had seen.

I tried to imagine things as they were two centuries ago here at this place, so violent then, so peaceful today. But I'm afraid my mental pictures were no sharper than the ranger's slide show. Maybe I'll go back another time and stand inside the walls of the star fort and try again to see.

# Roanoke Island—From Virginia Dare To The General Who Invented Sideburns

On THE MAP ROANOKE ISLAND is an unprepossessing place, an oblong area in Albemarle Sound squeezed between the Outer Banks and the Alligator River Wildlife Preserve, an anchor for the damp far eastern tip of US 64. The map shows two towns on the island, Manteo to the north and Wanchese to the south, with marshes separating them.

If you go to Roanoke you will find it to be what the map suggests, a low sandy island covered with pine trees and moss-draped live oaks. In season red and pink crepe myrtles line many streets in the towns. Even in summer, when tourists are thick on the ground, the local people are friendly. The pace of life on Roanoke is measured and quiet. It is hard to imagine the world-shaping events that happened there not so long ago.

The first stop for a visitor to the island should be the Fort Raleigh National Historic Site on the north shore just off US 64. A movie and exhibits there tell of Sir Walter Raleigh's first English colony in the new world, a bit of history that is familiar to most people. The story of the colony's brave little band vanishing in the mists of time has become a quaint legend. A visit to Roanoke brings the legend back to earth. Baby Virginia Dare and her parents were real people who had been abandoned in a trackless unknown wilderness. You can't hear their story without wondering.

Outside the visitor center is Fort Raleigh, a small sand fortification built by the colonists. Its site and shape have been determined from excavations made over the last century. Recent digging shows that near the fort was a metallurgical laboratory—the new world's first scientific endeavor—where one of the settlers, a German named Gans, sought mineral riches in the new world. Perhaps someday as archaeologists proceed with their work even the fate of the lost colony—and little Virginia—will be known. I hope so.

Close to Fort Raleigh are the Elizabethan Gardens, a large area of shaded walks, statuary, shrubs and flowers maintained since 1951 by the Garden Clubs of North Carolina. In the center of the area is the Sunken Garden, a formal arrangement of geometric beds done in the English fashion. Near the Garden is the Waterside Theater, where in summer Paul Greene's famous drama, The Lost Colony, is staged.

When you leave the gardens and the sixteenth century be ready to leap forward in time about three hundred years. Go back to the visitor center and ask the ranger at the desk about the Civil War on Roanoke Island, a story of invasion and battle as unlikely, to me, as the story of the lost colony.

The ranger will tell how on February 8, 1862 an armada of sixty-seven Union ships, after the capture of Confederate forts at Hatteras inlet, moved up the sound to Roanoke Island. After a lengthy artillery bombardment 13,000 Union soldiers landed in amphibious assault near the site of Raleigh's earlier settlement.

When you leave the visitor center make your way down to the shore near Fort Raleigh and close your eyes. Then open them and look out over narrow Croatan Sound. See the empty choppy waters, but see them crowded with ships and rowboats filled with blue-clad soldiers. Hear cannons roar and rifles crack. See the first rowboat crunch on the sand and the men climb out and run across the sand.

See it if you can. I couldn't.

In the two days that followed the invasion, Union forces overran the Confederate positions. Capture of Roanoke opened all of eastern North Carolina to the Union army and materially weakened the Confederate war capabilities.

The Union commander at Roanoke was General Ambrose Burnside, a bald giant of a man who let his whiskers grow down his cheeks. Burnside's whiskers in time became known as "sideburns," and a new word entered our language.

The ranger at the visitor center will show you on a map where, at low tide, remains of Confederate fortifications can be seen in the sound. Few Civil War excavations have been made, but bullets and cannon balls still turn up from time to time.

When you leave Fort Raleigh drive two miles further west on US 64 to Manteo and visit the new waterfront development with its shops and restaurants. Tour the Elizabeth II, a replica of a ship from Raleigh's time anchored near its visitor center across a channel from the waterfront. Try to picture yourself crossing the Atlantic Ocean in the quaint little toy boat!

Visit the North Carolina Aquarium on the shore of Croatan Sound west of Manteo. The modern facility is well-stocked and features special exhibits throughout the year.

You might want to drive the ten miles to Wanchese, a busy fishery town at the south end of the island, and have dinner at a seafood restaurant there. Or you can cross the bridge from Manteo over Roanoke Sound to the Outer Banks. Turn south there and you can explore the seventy miles of Cape Hatteras National Seashore with its lonely beaches and bird sanctuaries. Or you can turn north on the Outer Banks and visit Kitty Hawk and the Wright Museum. Or you can climb Jockey's Ridge dunes, or you can go fishing, or hang-glide or...

And, oh yes, as you move around the Roanoke area keep a sharp lookout for Andy Griffith, who lives there.

# Charleston—Little Brown Fleas And A Gray Whale

I STOOD WITH MY WIFE ON THE pier at Charleston's beautiful new Waterfront Park and looked out across the harbor toward Patriots Point and the looming mass of the aircraft carrier Yorktown. On the late May morning of our visit three tiny brown dots barely showed above the waterline near the Yorktown, like fleas nestling up to a gray whale.

The dots were the Nina, the Pinta and the Santa Maria, or authentic replicas thereof, which had arrived the day before at Charleston, a stop-off city on their Columbus-commemorating voyage from the old world to the new. Could there possibly be a more stunning example of the world's changes in the last half-millennium than Columbus's ships in the shadow of an aircraft carrier?

At ten o'clock the sun was warm but a cool breeze off the water kept us comfortable. Waterfront Park with its neat flower beds, swings, sculpture, green lawns and wading fountain is a popular spot. Already a number of people were there: obvious pale-skinned tourists, mothers pushing baby carriages, a scattering of business suits drinking their coffee break, and a few fishermen leaning out over the railings at the end of the pier. One man actually caught a large fish as I watched.

A hot dog vendor at his post near the fountain arranged his wares for later in the day. No one was wading in the fountain yet, but later in the day the shallow pool would be awash with squealing children, from toddlers to rambunctious big boys, and maybe a few senior citizens cooling their toes at the edge.

We left Waterfront Park to find our way across the harbor to Patriots Point. Two clip-clopping horse-drawn tourist wagons, both piloted down the middle of the street by young women dressed in old-Charleston garb, held us up briefly. The wagons were full. We could hear the guides with their megaphones describing sites and relating Charleston history as we passed. One guide was telling about Hurricane Hugo's visit to the city, still a frequent topic of conversation among Charlestonians, who are proud of all the high water marks on their buildings. But of course Charlestonians are proud of *everything* in their city.

We drove up Meeting Street, past Citadel Square, past the museum and huge new visitor center with its broad parking lot. Charleston is fully prepared to welcome you and many thousands like you. We turned onto US 17 and drove north across the two-span Cooper River bridge. A right turn shortly after the bridge brought us to the Yorktown.

When you visit Patriots Point be prepared to walk. The carrier is the length of three football fields. I don't know how tall the ship is, but of the six official tours you can take aboard her, one goes five decks down to the engine room and another seven decks up to the flight deck. So be prepared to climb as well as walk. All of the ups and downs are steep but most have two railings.

The Yorktown is the second aircraft carrier to bear the name. The first was sunk at the Battle of Midway. On the cavernous hangar deck which fills the middle of the ship exhibits of all kinds tell the history of both Yorktowns. A 1944 award-winning documentary movie, "The Fighting Lady," is shown on the hangar deck. The film, which consists mainly of actual battle scenes photographed from planes or ships during combat, evokes strongly the World War II era, particularly for those of us who lived through it.

Several smaller ships are permanently anchored with the Yorktown at Patriots Point: the nuclear ship, Savannah; the diesel submarine, Clamagore; a Coast Guard cutter; and a destroyer. All beckon you to explore them. Do so, but wear comfortable shoes and take your time. A great slice of our country's modern history is there to be seen and listened to.

After two hours wandering around the Yorktown and a walk-through of the Clamagore my wife and I calmly stepped back five centuries and went aboard the little wooden flea-ships. Whereas you could not explore all of the Yorktown in a week, you could stand in the center of the Nina and almost touch everything in the tub-shaped hull. To cross the harbor in it would seem a doubtful proposition to me. To launch out onto an uncharted ocean... I'll pay more attention to Mr. Columbus next time his day rolls around.

We left Patriot's Point and spent the afternoon leisurely strolling through Charleston's old town. We rested on breezy park benches or just leaned on the railing at the Battery and gazed across the harbor. After an exhausting morning on the Yorktown refighting World War II, a war fought far away from Charleston, we had decided to wait until the next day to visit Charleston's own historic forts. Tomorrow we would learn of times when the wars were not far away, but were fought right there where we were standing. Right there in soft, peaceful Charleston.

# A Tale Of Two Forts

I THINK OF CHARLESTON AS A
place of gentle horses pulling tourist wagons through shaded
streets, of old pastel-painted houses, of picture-book walled
gardens, of outdoor markets and friendly people—an easy-
going city, peaceful, quiet. It wasn't always so.

Momentous events of war, desperate battles that shaped
the future of our country—and of the world—took place in
Charleston in times not so very long ago. Visits to sites of
those battles, Fort Moultrie and Fort Sumter, should be at the
top of your Charleston to-see list. Go and stand where the
fighting happened. Look out over the water and try to
imagine.

On the hot morning of June 28, 1776, six days before
the Declaration of Independence was signed in Philadelphia,
a mixed force of Americans under Colonel William Moultrie
waited next to their cannons behind the soft palmetto logs of
a half-built fort on Sullivan's Island at the entrance to
Charleston harbor. They watched the methodical maneuvering
of a British fleet as it prepared to attack their fort and then
invade Charleston. The British armada, fifty ships under
command of Sir Peter Parker, had sailed from Ireland three
months earlier.

Heavy men-of-war flying the British flag moved to within
a quarter mile of the fort—point blank range—where they

turned their broadsides to the Americans, anchored and opened fire. Six regiments of British Redcoats from accompanying transports began landing on the beach to the north. Over the next few hours the British would send some 12,000 shot and shell crashing into Moultrie's fort. The fate of the southern colonies and of the just-begun American Revolution hung on the courage of the men behind those spongy palmetto logs.

Eighty-five years later, at 4:30 in the morning of April 12, 1861, a mortar shell arched across the Charleston sky and exploded with great flash and boom almost directly over Fort Sumter, a brick fort built on a sand bank in the harbor just a mile from Fort Moultrie. For the next thirty-four hours the Federal troops on Fort Sumter, under command of Major Robert Anderson, would endure constant bombardment from guns and mortars in Charleston and surrounding points. On April 14 Major Anderson surrendered to the Confederates. The next day President Lincoln called out 75,000 militia. The Civil War had begun.

To reach Fort Moultrie from Charleston you cross the Cooper River bridge, bear right past Patriots Point, then cross the causeway and bridge to Sullivan's Island. The fort is a mile to your right, on the south end of the island. Park your car at the large visitor center across the road from the actual fortifications.

A short film at the center portrays the history of the fort, from its beginning in Colonel Moultrie's defeat of the British fleet in 1776, through the Civil War and World Wars I and II, to its decommissioning as an active military post in 1947. Uniforms and equipment used by soldiers who manned the fort during each period are displayed.

Leave the visitor center and walk through—or climb over—sections of the fort refurnished as they were for each period of its service. Trace the development of coastal defense artillery from the muzzle loaders of Colonel Moultrie's time through the monster cannon of World War II. Before you leave Fort Moultrie, stand on a high point and look south across a narrow span of water to Fort Sumter.

Fort Sumter tour boats leave from several places in Charleston. My wife and I drove back from Sullivan's Island to Patriots Point and embarked from there on the good ship "Beauregard" bound for the fort. The boat ride cost $8 apiece and took a little more than a half hour each way. Points of interest in the harbor were described as we passed them. The Beauregard docked at the fort and remained there an hour. We were met by park rangers, who conduct guided tours of the site. If you prefer you may wander on your own.

From the fort's walls you can look across three miles of harbor to the Charleston Battery where much of the bombardment in 1861 originated. In the opposite direction from the Battery is Fort Moultrie. In Fort Sumter's interior an impressive museum with many contemporary photographs brings the bitter Civil War days to stark life.

The rangers shooed us back to the boat when our hour was up and, sobered from our quick glimpse of the violence and hardness of yesterday, we returned to Charleston to enjoy the peace and pleasantness of today and to think about the changes that have occurred in our world since Colonel Moultrie's time. During our Fort Sumter visit I had seen a particularly arresting example of those changes.

I was leaning on a muzzle-loading cast iron Civil War cannon looking across the water toward Fort Moultrie with its even older armament, when a nuclear submarine—today's

155

coastal defense gun—entered the channel between the forts and headed seaward. The long thin hull and tall conning tower slicing through the green harbor water—within range of the silent old guns of both forts—brought home to me in a way that reading never could a sense of the crunching march of history.

I wish that Colonel Moultrie and Major Anderson could have been there to see it with me.